Nicaragua:
A People's Revolution
BY THE EPICA TASK FORCE

DEDICATION TO "LOS MUCHACHOS" OF WASHINGTON D.C.

This primer on the Nicaraguan revolution has its roots in the relationships that developed between Nicaraguans and North Americans in Washington, D.C. during 1978 and 1979. An outgrowth of this solidarity movement and similiar ones organized after September 1978 in many cities throughout the United States, was the National Network in Solidarity with the Nicaraguan People, created in February 1979. The National Office of this Network was initially housed in EPICA's office and one of our staff served as the national coordinator for two months. This active participation in local and national solidarity work gave us direct knowledge of events in Nicaragua, providing the background and initiative for this publication.

At the forefront of the solidarity activities here in Washington, D.C. was a group of young Nicaraguans who had fled Somoza's repressive terror, and had organized the Washington Area Nicaraguan Solidarity Organization (WANSO). These committed Nicaraguans (affectionately called "*los muchachos*" or young people of Washington, D.C.) were our main connection with those *muchachos* or young people who were carrying forward the resistance within Nicaragua. Here in Washington, D.C., WANSO led marches through our streets and coordinated protests of institutions and individuals supporting the Somoza dictatorship. The words and actions of these Nicaraguan freedom fighters stirred our consciences, educated us politically, and inspired us to an ever-deepening solidarity with their liberation struggle.

We dedicate this primer, NICARAGUA: A PEOPLE'S REVOLUTION to these young Nicaraguans and to all "*los muchachos*" outside of Nicaragua whom they symbolized—a veritable international liberation brigade. Through their example, we in the United States—religious and solidarity groups, trade unions, student and women's organizations, and dedicated individuals—who added our contribution to the heroic struggle going on in Nicaragua were moved to a new level of anti-imperialist awareness, international solidarity and personal sacrifice. The unity thus forged between the North American and Nicaraguan peoples will not be broken, nor forgotten.

We hold a very special place in our hearts for our *companero* Enoc Ortez, who lived and worked with us here in the District of Columbia until he felt compelled to return to his people in Nicaragua. As a member of the FSLN, he died in battle in northern Nicaragua just a few short weeks before the victorious overthrow of Somoza. To Enoc and to all the Nicaraguans who gave their lives for the freedom of their people and their nation, we say "*Presente Companeros!*"

- *The EPICA Task Force*
  Yvonne Dilling
  Philip Wheaton
  Lisa Wheaton
  Christopher Conybeare

ABOUT THIS PRIMER

Our primary purpose in preparing this primer on the recent revolution in Nicaragua is to educate the North American public on the true nature of this historic struggle. This revolution was not primarily a battle between the repressive dictatorship of Anastasio Somoza and the leftist Sandinista Front for National Liberation (FSLN), nor was it a civil war between two opposing sectors of Nicaraguan society, as it has often been described. Rather, it was a struggle between the Somoza dynasty, which was supported by special U.S. interests, and the vast majority of the Nicaraguan people—a majority that cut across all class and economic lines.

To appreciate the unique character of this popular struggle to overthrow Somoza it is necessary to examine the makeup of the individual sectors of the Nicaraguan society as each as each took a turn leading and supporting the resistance. In this primer, we follow the ebb and flow of the critical events in Nicaragua between January 1978 and September 1979, on a month-by-month basis, beginning with the death of Pedro Joaquin Chamorro, carrying through to victory in July and concluding with the early developments of the Government of National Reconstruction. By describing and analyzing each of these sectors, we have attempted to weave a fabric of the whole revolutionary process as it developed, deepened and finally triumphed.

Our secondary purpose in writing this primer is to underscore the imperialist role of special U.S. interests during the long history of the Somoza dynasty. The North American people must come to grips with the exploitative goal of those economic interests (and also with the manipulative role of the reactionary individuals in the U.S. Congress and State Department) which, from beginning to end, supported the Somozas and financed the National Guard. Furthermore, the ambivalent position of the Carter administration during this recent period must be understood for what it was: an attempt to break from Somoza the man, while trying to keep the system representing Somoza interests (*somocismo*) intact. The price paid for this pro-*somocismo* position— 40,000 Nicaraguan lives lost, the physical destruction of six principal cities, and the total bankruptcy of an economy ($1.8 billion in debt)—is too high to gloss over or excuse under the banner of Carter's concern for human rights.

We hope this primer will open the hearts and sharpen the reflection of many North Americans so they may see the positive nature of this liberation struggle for the future of Nicaragua, as well as the warning it represents for the other repressive dictatorships in Central America. Our purpose is not to discredit our country as a freedom-loving people; to the contrary, our goal is to distinguish the American people from those international policies and economic strategies which only serve the interests of a very small and self-serving minority in the United States. By speaking the truth and by deepening our ties with the Nicaraguan people who are building a new society based on freedom and justice, we sincerely believe that we ourselves will become a more just nation and a more liberated people.

PROLOGUE

The successful overthrow of the Somoza dynasty and the defeat of the National Guard was made possible by and can only be understood through the integral relationship between the Nicaraguan people and the Sandinista Front for National Liberation (FSLN). On May 31, 1979, just prior to the final offensive against the dictatorship, one Nicaraguan analysis of that relationship stated:

That the people have chosen [the FSLN] is a profoundly impressive fact. If this were not true, one could not explain the growth and consolidation of the FSLN, nor the development of the popular revolutionary war in our country. The people are with the FSLN and the FSLN is with the people.

This description is profoundly true. In fact, in many ways, the two forces described were at times interchangeable. This does not mean they were indistinguishable. The FSLN was the armed vanguard of the sympathetic and militant civilian masses. But the two forces were interchangeable for a number of reasons: the civilians were continually joining the FSLN while the guerrillas were constantly working with the urban organizations; the masses were the supply and support forces for the Sandinista Front while the FSLN represented the potential of actually defeating the dictatorship. The two forces were not merely allies, but after September 1978 there was no serious ideological conflict between the people and their vanguard; and finally, not only did the FSLN lead and inspire the people but on a number of occasions the people led and inspired the FSLN.

Obviously, this relationship changed in many ways after July 19, 1979, when the building of a revolution began. In this primer, we only begin to describe this process in order to give the reader an introduction to the new government and the reconstruction process. But the point made above still holds true today: *the FSLN is the vanguard of both the great majority of the Nicaraguan people and of the Government of National Reconstruction.* In Nicaragua today, the roles and responsibilities of the FSLN, the people and the Government are in a process of dynamic interaction. They are struggling to bring organization and discipline to the people and to mobilize and rebuild a destroyed society and bankrupt economy. In the post-revolutionary period between July 1979 and early 1980, when this book went to press, all three forces were cooperating and impacting each other in a creative way. This dynamic relationship was described in the FSLN newspaper *Barricadas*, on August 4, 1979 in this manner:

The incredible worker and campesino *forces of our people who yesterday found themselves blocked by a dictatorial barrier, will now through the revolution have a fertile soil in which to organize, develop and strengthen themselves politically and ideologically and to move forward forging their indissoluble unity.... The political organization of Sandinismo, the Popular Sandinista Army and all our people [once] organized, will be the true guarantee of the fulfillment of this stage of our revolution.*

NICARAGUA: A PEOPLE'S REVOLUTION is the fruit of two years of labor by the EPICA Task Force in collaboration with the U.S.-based National Network in Solidarity with the Nicaraguan People, which supports the present Nicaraguan struggle to overcome past injustices and its right to self-determination in building a new society.

We express deep appreciation to Mary Jo Bowman for her major editorial work; to Lyn Barbee and Peggy Healy for their editorial assistance, textual advice and criticisms. We especially thank those Nicaraguans on the Embassy staff in Washington, D.C., who offered their perspectives and political clarifications, and those North Americans who provided the financial assistance that made this publication possible. Our gratitude also extends to EPICA staff members, Lisa Wheaton and Christoper Conybeare for their support throughout this project.

Finally, we thank all those Nicaraguans involved in the revolutionary process today, who, from Ocotal and Chinandega to Rivas and Penas Blancas, offered their time and hospitality to the EPICA staff during our September-October 1979 travels through their country. We particularly thank Doris Tijerino, of the FSLN Foreign Relations Secretariat; Carlos Fernando Chamorro, (then) official of the Ministry of Culture; and the comrades in **Casas Sandinistas** throughout Nicaragua. Without such committed companeros this project would not have been possible.

Philip Wheaton
Yvonne Dilling
co-authors

Art Direction by Liz Mestres
Typography by Keith Hefner
Cover photograph by Marcelo Montecino

Copyright © 1980
EPICA Task Force
ISBN 0918346-04-5
Printed in Washington D.C.

CONTENTS

Introduction
1 A Brief History of U.S. Imperialism and Class Relations in Modern Nicaragua
9 A Recent Contextual History: 1977

Part 1 January—December 1978
16 The Assassination of Pedro Joaquin Chamorro
18 Business Work Stoppage & Popular Unrest
20 Monimbo: Flame of Popular Resistance
23 Organizing the Campesinos: The ATC
26 Student Mobilization Against the Dictatorship
29 The Role of Women in the Revolution: AMPRONAC
32 The Consolidation of Popular Forces: The MPU
35 Attack on the National Palace
37 The September Insurrection of 1978
41 Nicaragua's Guernicas: National Guard Brutality & the Refugees
45 Organizing the Urban Masses: The CDC
46 The U.S. Mediation Effort & the Role of the FAO

Part 2 January 1979—Victory
52 National Patriotic Front: The People's Parallel Power Structure
54 Religious Mediation & Solidarity: The Role of the Church
57 The Reunification of the FSLN
59 Preparations for the Final Offensive
61 Provisional Government: Preventing Imperialist Intervention
63 Final Sandinista Offensive Against the Somoza Dynasty
69 People's Victory, Somoza's Vengeance

Part 3 Liberated Nicaragua: August—December 1979
76 The Somoza Legacy: Economic Bankruptcy
79 Sandinista Defense Committees: Popular Political Base
81 Agrarian Reform: Foundation of the Revolution
84 Labor Organizing: The ATC and CST
86 Rising Social & Political Problems
89 Popular Political Education
93 Mass Organizations: Youth and Women
96 New Foreign Policy: Non-Alignment

101 **Selected Bibliography**
102 **Glossary**

A Brief History of U.S. Imperialism & Class Relations in Modern Nicaragua

by Edmundo Jarquin C. and Pablo Emilio Barreto

The Death of Somoza

Somoza's death, like Foster's,
is a terrible loss, says Ike. Weep!
for the free world. "He was a great friend
of the United States, in public
and in private."
They'll have to enlarge Arlington
or fix up the White House Lawn
to bury their bosom buddies. And I bet
they're at it already. Because I looked for
Somoza's body all over Nicaragua,
and nobody knew what to say.
                    Ernesto Mejia Sanchez

North American intervention in Nicaragua began in 1912. It obstructed or retarded the process of developing a national state like those existing or emerging elsewhere in Central and South America. A foreign will—that of the United States—became the basis of political power, totally subordinating the liberal and conservative factions which made up the creole oligarchy.

In 1926, during a brief absence of direct U.S. military intervention, the conservative *caudillo*, General Emiliano Chamorro—the same man who had signed the Chamorro-Bryan canal pact—carried out a *coup d'etat*. Thus ended a long-standing political arrangement between liberals and conservatives imposed under North American influence in order to stabilize the country. In response to the *coup*, the liberals initiated what they called a "constitutionalist" war which first erupted along the Atlantic coast. Essentially, the liberals were demanding respect for the constitution which Chamorro had violated by denying the liberal leader and then Vice-President, Dr. Juan Bautista Sacasa, his right to presidential succession.

This liberal revolt, supported by the Mexican government (at that time in open conflict with the United States) rapidly spread through the whole country. Chamorro's conservative army was forced to retreat, thereby threatening to eliminate from political power that oligarchic faction which had been historically preferred by the United States. Alarmed by the civil war undermining its stabilization plan, and fearful of Mexican support for a liberal nationalist regime, the United States government once again militarily intervened to secure its *mare nostrum*.

The U.S. occupation army forced a dishonorable peace upon the victorious liberal army led by General José María Moncada, in exchange for guarantees of U.S. controlled elections to be held in 1928. In the meantime, the United States forced Chamorro to turn the presidency over to Adolfo Diaz—the same man the United States had installed

Chamorro

Moncada

as president after its first intervention in 1912. According to the arrangement imposed on General Moncada on May 4, 1927 (known as the Espino-Negro pact), Díaz would serve out the presidential term. Sacasa won the 1928 election and Moncada remained as head of the army. This arrangement instituted a period of "liberal" governments, but like the previous conservative administrations, it too would lack any genuine nationalist character.

But one man refused to accept the North American arrangement. General Augusto César Sandino, a commander in the liberal army under Moncada, led an armed rebellion protesting the unconstitutionality of the imposed Espino-Negro pact. Sandino's fundamental claim was to end U.S. presence in Nicaragua.

From that moment on, the country had a name around which to rally: Sandino, "General of Free Men."* With his army of peasants supported by patriotic sectors in the cities, Sandino launched an heroic guerilla war that lasted from 1927 until 1933. Although Sandino's army was never able to defeat the growing and increasingly sophisticated U.S. forces, the war finally forced the United States to withdraw its troops. Faced with the impossibility of defeating Sandino and with the rising tide of international solidarity with the national hero, the U.S. government redefined its political strategy. Before leaving Nicaragua, it developed a new plan of political stabilization. The key to this new plan was the creation of a Nicaraguan National Guard that would act as a replacement army for the U.S. Marines. Through this scheme, the North Americans sought to erode the political and ideological base of the Sandino struggle by setting Nicaraguans (the National Guard) against Nicaraguans (Sandino's army).

When the U.S. Marines pulled out of Nicaragua on January 1, 1933 the United States left behind a legally constituted and fully trained National Guard under the leadership of Anastasio Somoza Garcia. General Somoza had lived in the United States and through his fluency in English and personal friendships with some of the Americans, was able to win their confidence. He then negotiated a *peace* between General Sandino and President Sacasa, a weak and vacillating leader. Sandino was wary, but since his prerequisite demand of the expulsion of the hated U.S. forces had been fulfilled, he agreed to a cease fire.

These peace arrangements opened up the possibility for an act of treason which would accomplish through cowardice what could not be accomplished in combat. On February 21, 1934, Sandino attended a dinner in Managua held by Sacasa at the Presidential Palace. Following the supper, Sandino, unarmed and without a bodyguard, was taken prisoner by Somoza and summarily executed. Immediately, an order went out for the extermination of the now-disarmed Sandinista army in the northern part of the country, where Sandino's followers, confident that peace was being arranged, awaited the return of their leader. Somoza's order resulted in what has come to be called "the first massacre of Wiwilí."

Nicaragua seen from the sky, the Yankees along the roads. Marti went up to the mountains with General Sandino.

Managua seen from the clouds.

Blood spilled in rebel towns of San Salvador. Marti has fallen.

Managua seen from Managua. The Marines have gone at last. The Yankees signed the treaty but they killed Sandino first.
   Rafael Alberti

A DICTATORSHIP "MADE IN THE USA"

With the assassination of General Sandino in 1934 and the subsequent *coup d'etat* against President Sacasa in 1936, Somoza García initiated the longest, most corrupt dictatorship in Latin American history, a dictatorship continually supplied and supported by the United States.

Sustained by his family's monopolistic control of the economy and by the military power of the National Guard, the Somoza dictatorship passed through several stages. Until the mid-1940's, the dictator held relative legitimacy among those sectors of the society who, in their own self-interest, cloaked their leader with an image of "pacifier" and "innovator." By the mid-1940's, Somoza's intentions to establish himself in perpetuity became clear, thus betraying the nationalist recovery goals of the Liberal Party, which Somoza now dominated. Furthermore, because of the democratic surge developing in Central America (emerging from the struggle against fascism during World War II), Somoza entered a period of total isolation. The dictatorship lost its legitimacy and maintained its control only through the coercion and power of the National Guard. By this time large numbers of liberals abandoned Somoza and formed the Independent Liberal Party, which together with the Conservative Party, subsequently constituted a solid bloc of opposition against the dictatorship.

Once the crisis of the second half of the 1940's had

Laying the groundwork for the U.S.-supported dynasty. Anastasio Somoza Garcia (front right) at a 1928 Thanksgiving meal hosted by General Jose Maria Moncada and attended by prominent U.S. Marine officers.

passed, a new stage developed. Worldwide economic recovery in the postwar period and technological developments in the area of agricultural chemicals facilitated the development of cotton cultivation. The rapid expansion of cotton production gave Nicaragua a primarily agrarian export economy. The resulting profits had a major impact on the overall economy, extending and diversifying the productive potential of the country.

Based primarily on cotton production and secondarily on the expansion of coffee and beef exports, significant economic growth led to the rapid modernization of the economy. Capital accumulation, mainly agrarian based, was transferred to other economic sectors such as industry, finance and commerce. This new wealth was dominated by the Somoza family which had become synonomous with "the State." With this control over the expansion and diversification process, Somoza greatly increased his impact upon the social life of the country.

As a result of these economic changes, new social sectors emerged while others rapidly deteriorated. Cotton cultivation, developed primarily in the departments of Managua, Masaya and along the West coast, accelerated a process of concentrating vast agrarian properties into a few hands. This same process converted large numbers of small farmers into plantation peasants and produced a significant migration of other *campesinos* off the land. These migrants converged particularly on the cities of the Pacific coast (León and Chinandega) and on Managua the capital, overloaded the urban employment market and put a tremendous strain on the weak social service structures (housing, schools, hospitals). This created those sociological imbalances commonly called "marginalization."

At the same time, because of the expansion of employment in the industrial, financial and state bureaucracy sectors, a new salaried middle class emerged. Social and economic success came to this middle class so rapidly that it failed to question the roots of its development. This created, intentionally or not, a new social strata which legitimized the dictatorship. This strata together with the emerging capitalist class—the cotton producers who also were completely dependent on the financial and technical assistance apparatus of the State—further strengthened Somoza's political control.

Despite the growing political legitimation by these new and ascending sectors, the vitality of the traditional liberal-conservative conflict was sustained during the 1950's. The conservative oligarchy maintained its economic independence from the State with the production and sale of coffee and beef inside and outside the country. This translated into their political autonomy from the Somoza regime.

In 1956 the founder of the dynasty was killed by a young poet and patriot, Rigoberto López Pérez. Following Somoza Garcia's death a conflict developed between the traditional opposition and Somoza's sons during the election campaign to select his successor. At that moment United States Ambassador Whelan came to the rescue of the dynasty by giving total support to the succession of the

Anastasio II, "tacho" (in dark glasses) and Luis (in dark suit) with U.S. Ambassador Whelan (far right) following the death of Somoza Garcia, founder of the dynasty.

dynasty through Luis Somoza Debayle, Anastasio's eldest son.

The creation of the Central American Common Market in the early 1960's stimulated the process of industrialization and thus accelerated the pace of modernization. However, this industrial expansion did not lead to any independence from Somoza. The state bureaucracy and the agrarian-export market, which developed at a parallel pace with industry, kept the Somoza interests in control of this expansion. The exploitative agrarian structure remained untouched, however, and this weakened the potential for industrial expansion.

> **The seed of Sandino's blood
> lashes the murderous rooftops;
> multiplied, in torrents
> it will cover exposed rooftops;
> and will insure, inevitable apocalypse.
> It will exterminate all of the murderers,
> and each and every one
> of the murderers' seed.**
>
> **Their treacherous embrace of Sandino
> is pregnant with biblical premonitions
> like the crime of Cain
> like the kiss of Judas.**
>
> **And then peace will reign...
> and Nicaragua will fill with olive branches and voices
> that loft to the heavans
> an everlasting psalm of love.**
>
> **Rigoberto Lopez Perez
> patriot and executioner of Anastasio I**

HISTORY WILL NEVER FORGIVE YOU

But history creates its own contradictions. The Somoza model of growth during the two previous decades, while producing wealth, modernization and political consolidation, also produced incredible social injustices and inequalities. As both the old and new social elites enriched themselves and prospered under Somoza, broad sections of the population became ever poorer and were swallowed up by the most brutal misery.

Urban development was incapable of absorbing the growing unemployed work force that emerged from natural

"Tacho" Somoza Debayle succeeded his brother, Luis, to the presidency in 1967.

Peasant family in plantation barracks in the Chinandega region.

At the same time, the portion of Nicaraguan capital in the Conservative Party was finally forced into dependency upon the State apparatus (i.e., upon Somoza) because all industry in Nicaragua functioned under the control of the State through its fiscal, credit and commercial concessions and privileges. The conservative faction, unable to gain control over this apparatus through election, rebellion or *coup d'etat*, could only obtain services from the state apparatus through coming to an *understanding* with Somoza. This ended the independence of the conservatives and thus the vitality of the old liberal-conservative conflict. This *understanding* was formalized in a pact between the conservative leader, Fernando Agüero and President Anastasio Somoza Debayle (Tacho), who inherited the dynasty following the death of his brother Luis in 1967. The pact was the product of the increasing concentration of control by those few economic groups in the parasitic bureaucracy linked to Somoza.

The decade of the 1960's was, without doubt, the period of Somoza's greatest power and social legitimation. The expanding State apparatus and the growing economy gave Somoza an unprecedented degree of influence among the upper class sectors—through coercion, blackmail and fraud. His secure position was guaranteed by the accumulation of family assets, multiple links with North American capital, and close associations with the Central American bourgeoisie, a factor that consolidated his borders. And, when none of these factors was able to resolve any domestic controversy, there was always the National Guard.

population growth as well as from the enormous migration of people expelled from the land. Within the poor rural population, a third of the *campesinos* were landless while another third subsisted on tiny farm plots located on marginally-productive land. Administrative corruption—induced and encouraged by the dictatorship—prevented an adequate or planned expansion of social services, despite a growing economy and increased foreign investment.

This increasingly unequal distribution of wealth placed a brake on the expansion potential of the internal market and in turn on the growth of the entire economy. Despite agrarian and industrial diversification, Nicaragua's economy continued to depend largely on exported agricultural products which suffered from constantly fluctuating world prices.

Nicaragua's 20 cordoba bill carried a photograph of Somoza and U.S. Ambassador Shelton.

In summary, these inequalities represented a profound and growing social contradiction on top of an extremely fragile model of growth. These two factors ultimately precipitated the irreversible crisis of the Somoza dictatorship.

THE STRUGGLE AGAINST THE DICTATORSHIP

Despite the expanding control of the dictatorship, a pro-democratic spirit persisted in the country—holding fast to its goals of justice and freedom.

This spirit was present in all the rebellions, resistance, protests and martyrdoms of young people from 1959 onward, including the struggle of the Sandinista Front for National Liberation (FSLN).

The weakening of the liberal-conservative conflict which became obvious during the second half of the 1960's created a political vacuum that was not immediately filled by the FSLN. While the FSLN was accumulating experience, the Sandinistas remained politically and strategically isolated. But the reformist tendencies also lacked a social base from which to fill this vacuum. The middle class, where such reforms traditionally arise, did not recognize the crisis because it was caught up in the process of social and economic self-improvement.

Gradually, the contradictions in the model of economic and social growth created the conditions for a final crisis of the dynasty. The struggle for freedom and justice emerged out of new organizational molds, with new content and perspectives, and with a greater intensity than ever seen before in Nicaragua. These forms began to appear after 1972.

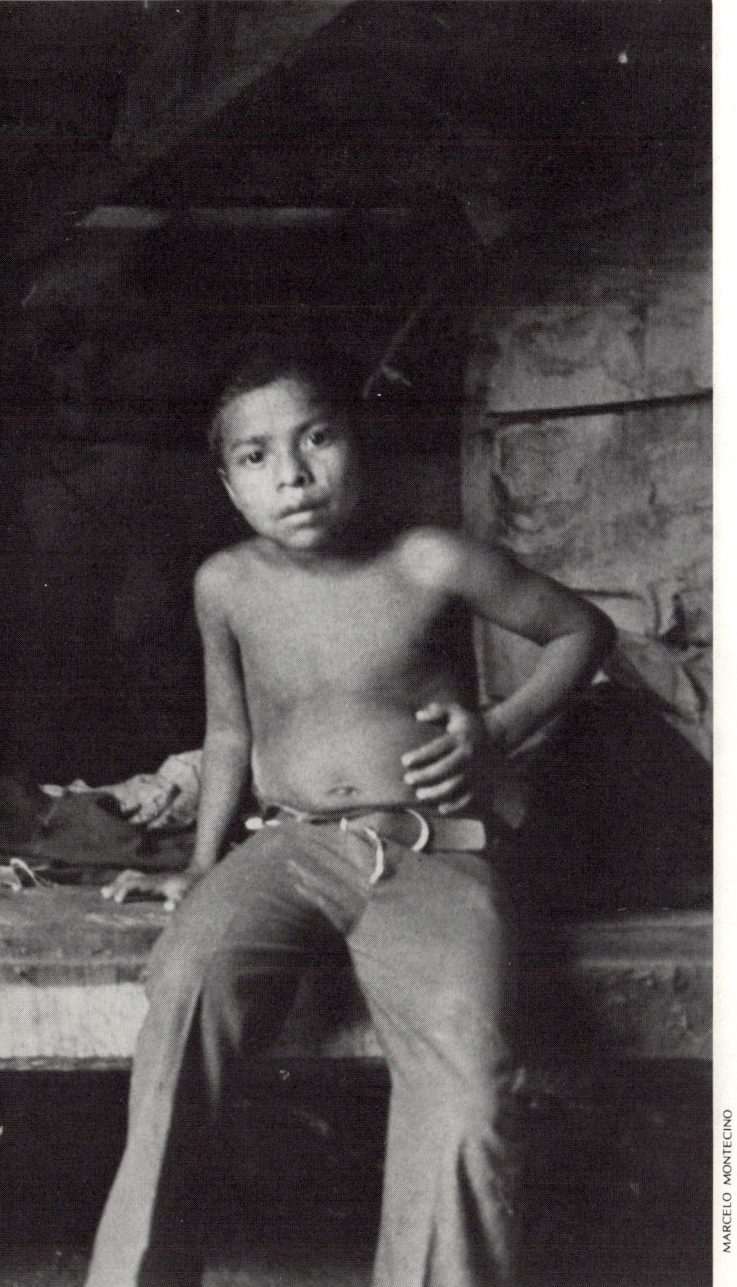

THE CRISIS ON THE MARCH

The crisis in the Central American Common Market—precipitated by the armed conflict between Honduras and El Salvador in 1969—coincided with a decline in international prices for primary agricultural and beef products. Together, these two factors induced a marked deceleration in the level of economic growth and a decline in the level of private investment.

Somoza was unable to adjust to the economic crisis. He tried to compensate for this decline through increased public spending, but his methods only increased unemployment while decreasing real income, especially of the popular sectors. This led to economic stagnation in general.

Then, in December 1972, an earthquake destroyed a large part of Managua. But, despite its tragic human consequences—10,000 died and over 100,000 were dislocated—the quake actually stimulated the economy. The destruction of housing, buildings, roads, furniture, and inventories created new opportunities for investment and production to replace the items lost. In addition, a huge influx of international public and private funds for reconstruction and insurance created the financing needed for the new investments. When this influx of funds was followed by favorable prices for sugar and beef in 1974-75 and for coffee in 1975, a significant reactivation of the Nicaraguan economy occurred.

However, the earthquake and its consequences led to a profound conflict between the bureaucratic bourgeoisie (Somoza and his friends) and the traditional bourgeoisie. The Somoza bloc, sustained by State power, exacerbated the existing administrative corruption by excluding other sectors of the bourgeosie from the opportunities for investment created by the earthquake. Somoza enriched himself personally in the process by organizing his own bank, insurance company, finance and construction firms. Overstepping the traditional ethical bounds of capitalist competition, Somoza took over the most dynamic areas of capital accumulation.

At the same time, the government's failure to respond to the critical needs of the people following the earthquake precipitated a crisis of support among the middle class and especially among the masses of suffering poor. The exaggerated administrative corruption had led to an alarming decline in the level of public administration. The government's inability to adequately administer the reconstruction process increased the already sharp social inequalities. In turn, Somoza's failure to act, coupled by his selfish exploitation of the quake, led to a widespread political radicalization of the people.

Given this fraud, and in order to finance some post-quake reconstruction, Somoza borrowed large sums of money, leading to a sharp increase in foreign indebtedness. This practice, in time, further reduced the dictator's space for

Downtown Managua in ruins following the 1972 earthquake. The destroyed sector was never rebuilt during the ensuing seven years of the dictatorship.

political and economic maneuvering. Incurring debts, by itself, might not be questionable if the new funds are destined to finance productive investments which will generate income to repay the loans. But such borrowing is dubious when it is done at such an accelerated rate (from $200 million dollars at the beginning of 1973 to $800 million by the end of 1977) and on the basis of repayment terms that are incompatible with the development projects supposedly being financed. Above all, such borrowing is suspect when the institutions that are to administer the foreign debt (such as Somoza's *Banco de Vivienda* and *Instituto de Fomento Nacional*) are inefficient, dishonest and already without capital assets as a result of corruption.

But to fully understand the depth of Somoza's crisis one must also look at the other significant developments of the post-quake period. First, as a result of Vatican Council II, and the Latin American Episcopal Conference in Medellin in 1968, the Catholic church had been redefining its goals and reorganizing its hierarchy. This was particularly true of the church in Nicaragua. This process led to a gradual divorce of the church from the dictatorship, especially as Somoza lost public support. Initially, the church only reduced its official support of Somoza, but later it began to take overt actions challenging the regime.

Second, in the strictly political arena, organizational and ideological opposition to the dictatorship arose from the non-traditional parties. In December 1974, the Democratic Union of Liberation (UDEL) was created, led by Pedro Joaquín Chamorro. UDEL represented a broadly pluralistic convergence of political forces, including conservatives, liberal democrats, Christian and social democrats, and even the Nicaraguan Socialist Party. These forces united around a platform calling for the recovery of democratic rights and a social and economic transformation of the society.

In addition, the Sandinista Front was becoming more closely associated with the struggle for democratic renewal, and especially with the immediate problems and demands of the masses. Towards this end, the FSLN established bases among the people which in time helped the organization overcome its political and strategic isolation.

Finally, with the ascendency of the Carter administration, the dimension of human rights appeared as a new strategy in North American politics. Whether or not this strategy implied any fundamental change towards Latin American problems, the overwhelming proof and continued denunciations of human rights violations in Nicaragua weakened the support of Somoza by the U.S. government—the creator and patron of the dictatorship during its entire existence. Thus, the United States relationship passed from one of unconditional support for Somoza to one that took on an ambiguous stance.

Introduction excerpted from "Recorrido a Travez de la Opresion, la Miseria...y la Lucha," in 44 Anos de Dictadura Somocista, *by Edmundo Jarquin C. and Pablo Emilio Barreto. Translated by EPICA.*

A Recent Contextual History 1977

"As long as Nicaragua has sons and daughters that love her, Nicaragua will be free."
                                    Augusto Cesar Sandino

— SANDINO AND HIS STAFF —
The Guerrilla Leader Is the Second Figure From the Left

HISTORY OF THE FSLN

The Sandinista Front for National Liberation (FSLN) was founded on July 26, 1961 in Honduras by Carlos Fonseca Amador, Tomás Borge and Silvio Mayorga. Carlos Fonseca argued that the "National Liberation Front" had to include the term "Sandinista" in its title because "Sandino had not only struggled against the North American intervention but had also outlined a concrete political program which was still viable within our present reality."[1] Even beyond this, according to Fonseca, there is a need to study and "resurrect" Sandino's entire perspective.[2]

Inspired by the Cuban model of guerilla warfare, the FSLN initially operated (1961-62) as mountain-based guerilla bands along the Honduran-Nicaraguan border. But military failures and hardships resulting from its clashes with the National Guard and Honduran army units, as well as the harshness of the mountain terrain, led to numerous deaths and desertions. The second phase focused on political activity in the city and included an alliance with the traditional left in Nicaragua, particularly with the Nicaraguan Socialist Party (the name used by the Communist Party) and the Republican Mobilization Organization. During this period, the FSLN concentrated its work in poor *barrios* using urban organizing committees. But by 1967, when the left parties joined the liberals and conservatives in

"Today the sunrise ceased to be a temptation." Carlos Fonseca Amador

electoral politics, the FSLN broke from the alliance and returned to the mountains, "organizing the guerilla group called Pancasán."[3]

The military defeat suffered by the Pancasán guerrillas (some 20 out of 35 members were killed) was, nonetheless, a political turning point in the history of the FSLN. From that point on, the Sandinista Front decided to carry out its armed struggle inside Nicaragua and, more importantly, with the people. As a result of that decision, the FSLN set up a new structure involving "intermediate organizations" as links to student, worker, Christian and cultural groups which became the "umbilical cord" between the Sandinista Front and the people. At the same time (around 1970), the FSLN began incorporating *campesinos* into its ranks and leadership. These new developments were part of a strategy called "the accumulation of forces in silence,"[4] a period that lasted from 1967 to 1974.

This silence was broken in December 1974 with an FSLN attack on the residence of Dr. Castillo Quant, led by the Juan José Quezada commando group. Until that date, armed attacks by the Sandinista Front had been largely defensive in nature—to physically survive and to gather weapons. The spectacular success of the December action[5] resulted in the recruitment of many new combatants. It was this rapid expansion that led to the emergence of the factions within the FSLN.

From 1975 on, an internal struggle developed between those who believed that the resistance to the dictatorship would require a "prolonged popular war" which would necessarily imply a permanent military base in the mountains (the Guerra Popular Prolongada or GPP tendency) versus those Sandinistas who beleived that the FSLN had to base itself primarily among the working class (the Proletarian or TP tendency). Tomas Borge clarified the GPP position:

In practice, we believed in the need to intensify our work among the workers in the centers of production. But we also maintained very firmly the need to keep the guerilla forces in the mountains. It was out of these positions that what could be called the first contradiction emerged."[6]

Thus, the two thrusts should not be seen as mutually exclusive, and indeed, the main strategy during 1974-75 was for a "continuation" of both armed struggle and political action.[7]

In late 1975 the GPP sanctioned the Proletarian tendency, although the TP refused to accept this disciplinary action. As Borge explains:

We (the GPP) said that all (such differences) could be discussed, but because at the same moment a number of disciplinary mistakes occurred, we applied certain measures, sanctions. And those sanctions were interpreted as a reprisal of the (new) political positions that were developing.[8]

The formation of the FSLN gave rise to new hope in Nicaragua.

These differences of emphasis did contain, however, some fundamental variants in them. Jaime Weelock, for instance, defined the TP position:

Within our Organization (the FSLN) there arose a group of us companeros who took the position that economic and political conditions in Nicaragua required more than a simple guerilla column or a university student organization that was more or less radicalized. The Organization, as the vanguard of the working class and the leader of all of our people against the military dictatorship, had to be from that class.[9]

Another factor leading to this division within the FSLN was the mounting repression by Somoza's National Guard under the state of siege imposed following the December 1974 action. Somoza also began using CONDECA forces (Council for the Defense of Central America)[10] to help the Guard wipe out the armed FSLN units in the northern part of the country. These forces included troops from Nicaragua, Guatemala, El Salvador and Honduras, as well as U.S. military advisors from the Panama Canal Zone. One of these operations, "Aguila Sexta" (Winter 1975-76) resulted in the death of many FSLN militants, forcing many others into exile, particularly to Mexico, Costa Rica and Panama.

In exile, the third tendency, called the "Insurrectionalists" took on concrete form. The Insurrectionalists differed from the other tendencies in their belief that Somoza was inherently weak. From this they concluded that bold attacks against the National Guard from outside Nicaragua would quickly damage his weak image, that popular uprisings inside the country were feasible, and that by holding a more pluralistic political line they could win the support of movements and governments antagonistic to Somoza. As Borge describes the situation:

This divergence was based on differences between those Sandinista leaders within Nicaragua and those who found themselves outside the country at that time. Those inside applied sanctions against the TP [also inside] while those outside opposed such sanctions. The Insurrectionalists had a third view on this conflict, and speaking generally, that is how they came to be called terceristas.[11]

Thus while it was the issue of the GPP sanctions against the TP that triggered the splitting into tendencies, their different views on strategy did lead to a questioning of political line. And this led to differences in practice that made it harder to resolve the conflict.

In the long run, the analysis and strategy of each of the tendencies were valid; a fact that strengthened the FSLN by broadening its perspectives. Despite these differences, the tendencies never formed distinct organizations and each considered itself to be both Sandinista in spirit and structurally part of the FSLN. As Borge said, "There were never serious ideological differences between us. The differences have been essentially of a political and strategic nature."[12]

THE EVENTS FROM JULY TO DECEMBER 1977

The rapidly developing systemic crisis in Nicaragua, outlined in the previous history, came to a head in relation to a personal crisis. On July 25, 1977, Anastasio Somoza suffered a mild heart attack. He was immediately flown to Miami where he remained under treatment for five weeks.[1]

Although he returned on September 7, presumably "completely recovered"[2] with some sectors of the Catholic church praying for his health, his absence and condition had triggered a series of speculations and political moves, including some challenging Somoza's leadership within his own Liberal Party.[3]

Perhaps to counter the negative rumors, in mid-September Somoza lifted the state of siege (martial law and press censorship) in effect since 1974.[4] This move toward liberalization only freed the opposition to re-initiate its campaign against the dictator. *La Prensa* (the main opposition newspaper) announced that the State had been forced to borrow 437 million *cordobas* from Somoza's Institute for National Development (INFO-NAC) to cover its foreign debts.[5] At the same time, it became public knowledge that the Social Security Institute was in a "disastrous" financial state, that the Power & Light Company (ENALUF) was without sufficient funds to operate, and that $c300,000 had disappeared from the Bank of America.[6]

Apparently, pressure from the United States had also influenced Somoza's decision to lift the state of siege. The U.S. Secretary of State for Latin America, Warren Christopher, had declared that the United States could only insure Nicaragua further military credit if civil rights liberties and human rights violations improved.[7] Pressing on this initiative for human rights, both the Social Christian Party and UDEL in early October demanded an end to the dictatorship and reinstatement of popular democracy.[8] UDEL outlined five conditions for the effectiveness of such a process: the removal of press censorship, trade union freedom, the designation of a non-Somoza official to head the National Guard, political pluralism, and amnesty for political prisoners.[9] By mid-October, Nicaragua's gathering economic crisis was being joined by rising political unrest.

Then, on October 12, a group of well-armed Insurrectionalist guerillas carried out a night attack on a police barracks in Ocotal in northern Nicaragua. The next night, another guerilla band successfully attacked the National Guard barracks in San Carlos on the Costa Rican border.[10] Two more FSLN actions were then carried out in central Nicaragua on the 17th and 18th in Masaya and Managua, respectively.[11] Immediately, the Guard reinforced and tightened its military patrol over all highways, reinstating a surveillance which had been relaxed when the state of siege was lifted. These attacks by the Sandinista Front not only created internal pressures on Somoza but, because he blamed them on the fact that Costa Rica and Honduras were harboring FSLN troops, tensions developed with these neighboring governments. In addition, the Mexican government sent a sharp criticism to Somoza when a National Guard official tried unsuccessfully to kidnap a group of Sandinistas who had taken refuge in the Mexican embassy in Managua.[12]

Sandinistas in an FSLN mountain training camp.

The October attacks by the FSLN sent shock waves through the Somoza regime because the FSLN was supposedly "virtually eliminated" following the training operations carried out during the Winter of 1976-77 by the CONDECA forces. The reappearance of the FSLN, now operating with more modern weapons and carrying out hit-and-run raids, made it clear to the government as well as the public that the FSLN was alive and growing stronger.

At the same time, a highly respected group of liberals calling themselves "The Twelve" began demanding substantial changes in the government. The government soon declared "The Twelve" guilty of criminal acts when they stated that the FSLN had matured politically and should be considered a legitimate part of the opposition.[13] As a result of this challenge and reaction, Archbishop Obando y Bravo called Somoza and the opposition to a "constructive dialogue."[14] This led UDEL to officially invite all opposition parties to participate in such a dialogue, a move supported by the influential economic organization INDE. To effect this discussion, Archbishop Obando was designated head of the Commission to Promote a National Dialogue.[15] But the FSLN declared that such a dialogue made sense only if and when Somoza left power.

Somoza responded to these peaceful suggestions by unleashing a new reign of repression against the people, especially in the countryside, hoping thereby to cut off *campesino* support and supply of the FSLN. As a result of this repression, during the six-week period (mid-October to the end of November) hundreds of *campesinos* disappeared, some of whom were tortured and others dropped from helicopters in remote regions of the country.[16] In the face of this new wave of terror a Permanent Commission on Human rights in Nicaragua (CPDH) along with AMPRONAC and student groups began to protest the disappearance of *campesinos*.[17]

These symbolic acts of protest gradually spread and soon involved broader sectors of the society. For example, in December the inhabitants of a poor development project called OPEN 3 carried out a vocal street rally which led to urban repression by the National Guard and then to many arrests. And in reaction to the OPEN 3 suppression, 6,000 hospital workers threatened to walk out along with the workers at the textile factory AGROTEX.[18] Each military reaction to a popular uprising triggered yet another protest, as the social anger throughout the country mounted.

In light of these events, "The Twelve" withdrew from the Dialogue forcing UDEL to issue a statement which read:

Given recent events, the agreement by the Government to dialogue is but a formal gesture, since it is not only postponing such a conversation but has continued implementing its repressive measures, both political and economic, against different sectors of the citizenry."

• *La Prensa*, Dec. 10, 1977

In December, Nicaragua's economic crisis exploded in a series of exposés of national fraud. The former Minister of Education charged that 3 million *cordobas* had disappeared from a fund designated for school construction;[19] the Congress authorized the Institute for Campesino Wel-

F.A.N. Fuerza Armada Nicaraguense, Somozas airforce.

fare (INVIERNO) to transfer 4 million *cordobas* to ENALUF, not only robbing Peter to pay Paul, but taking funds from the rural poor to keep the cities solvent;[20] the Chamber of Engineers and Architects accused the National District of "disloyal competition" because it gave a North American firm a contract for building roadways in Managua;[21] Somoza's son illegally took funds from the public treasury to construct buildings for his Basic Training School for the Infantry (EEBI);[22] Somoza himself appropriated 25 million *cordobas* to build an airport for himself on his private farm)[23] and the Nicaraguan Chamber of Builders announced its discovery that the Housing Bank (owned by Somoza) had used 204 million *cordobas* to "finance social interests" and another 279 million for "mortgage loans to particular parties."[24] The years of Somoza's outright stealing and manipulation of federal funds were becoming public at the moment of greatest political challenge to the dynasty.

In late December, UDEL announced its pre-conditions for any dialogue with the government:

1. A broad investigation of the disappearance of the *campesinos*.
2. Freedom for all prisoners not charged with specific crimes.
3. Exhaustive investigation of the use of public funds by government agencies.
4. Suspension of arbitrary actions against radio and TV stations.
5. End to all interruption of political activities by opposition organizations.
6. Rights demanded by numerous labor unions.
7. The end to all persecution of "The Twelve."[25]

After these demands were published in *La Prensa*, Somoza's newspaper, *Novedades* charged *La Prensa* editor Pedro Joaquin Chamorro with trying "to block the good proposals (of the "Dialogue") in order to stir up a fire of violence against the true desires of the Nicaraguan people."[26] In response, *La Prensa* challenged the dictator, stating "Somoza has the next word."[27] A few days later Chamorro was assassinated.

FOOTNOTES

History of the FSLN
1. Daniel Waksman Schinca, "Interview with Tómas Borge", *El día,* Mexico City, April 17, 1979, p. 22
2. EDUCA, *El Pensamiento Vivo De Sandino,* San José, Costa Rica, 1974. Most of Sandino's thought is contained in his Letters written between 1927-1933.
3. Daniel Waksman S., April 18, 1979 "Interview" part II. p. 22
4. Daniel Waksman S., p. 22
5. "Diciembre Victorioso"
6. Daniel Waksman S., p. 22
7. The word used in Spanish was "continuidad".
8. Daniel Waksman S., p. 22
9. Jaime Wheelock, *Causa Sandinista,* No. 5, Tendencia Proletaria, Nov. 1978, San Jose, Costa Rica, p. 4
10. CONDECA is a creation of the Inter-American Defense Board, originally formed in the late 1950's by the United States as a cooperative counter-insurgency potential. The Board is located in Washington, D.C.
11. Daniel Waksman S., p. 22

The Events from July to December 1977
1. *Novedades,* July 25, 1977
2. *Novedades,* July 29, 1977
3. *La Prensa,* October 3 & 5, 1977
4. *La Prensa,* Sept. 9, 1977
5. *La Prensa,* Sept. 27, 1977
6. *Encuentro: La Realidad Nacional,* Universidad Centroamericana, No. 14, July-Dec. 1978, p. 8
7. *Encuentro,* p. 9
9. *La Prensa,* Sept. 24, 26, 27 & 28, '77
10. *La Prensa,* Oct. 10, 1977
11. *La Prensa,* Oct. 19, 1977
23. *La Prensa,* Oct. 22, 1977
13. *La Prensa,* Nov. 1, 5 and 19, 1977.
14. *La Prensa,* Oct. 10, 1977
15. *La Prensa,* Nov. 30, 1977
16. *Encuentro,* p. 12
17. *Encuentro,* p. 12
18. *La Prensa,* Dec. 10, 1977
19. *La Prensa,* Dec. 1, 2, 15, 1977
20. *La Prensa,* Dec. 1, 1977
21. *La Prensa,* Dec. 23, 1977
22. *La Prensa,* Dec. 22, 1977
24. *La Prensa,* Dec. 13, 1977; *Novedades,* Dec. 11, '77
25. Signed Dec. 28, 1977; *Encuentro,* p. 14
26. *Novedades,* Jan. 6, 1978
27. *La Prensa,* Jan. 6, 1978

Poem translations on pages 1, 2, and 4 taken from Nicaragua: Song and Struggle, *a publication of the Nicaragua Solidarity Committee of Minnesota.*

Nicaragua: A People's Revolution

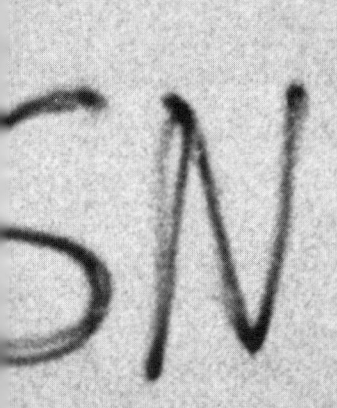

PART 1
January - December 1978

THE ASSASSINATION OF PEDRO JOAQUIN CHAMORRO

LA PRENSA

The beginning of the visible downfall of the Somoza dynasty can be directly linked to the assassination of Pedro Joaquin Chamorro on January 10, 1978. That morning Pedro Joaquin drove alone to work, as usual, through the desolate earthquake zone of old Managua. Suddenly two cars overtook him and forced him to stop; its occupants climbed out and fired at point blank range. Chamorro died instantly; his body had been perforated with 30 gunshot wounds, according to the doctors at the Oriental Hospital where the corpse was first taken. From there, his body was carried back to his home in a seven-hour pre-funeral procession of some 50,000 persons. As time and events were to prove, "You can't assassinate all of them."[1]

The next day, even larger crowds attended the funeral, marking the growing national chorus of outrage. Simultaneously, large bands of protesters attacked business establishments along Managua's Carretera Norte including the Central American Bank, the Customs Office, a branch of First National City Bank. Particularly hard hit was the office of a blood-purchasing business called Plasmaferesis. This focus of the people's wrath was not accidental. Pedro Ramos, a Cuban exile based in Miami and head of Plasmaferesis, was accused by one of the assassins, Silvio Peña Rivas, as being the intellectual author of the crime.[2] Another Plasmaferesis business advisor, a North American named Frank Kelly, was a close friend of Somoza. Also implicated were Noel Pallais Debayle and Lillian Somoza de Sevilla Sacasa, relatives of the dictator, and Colonel Bayardo Jirón, executive director of Somoza's Office of Security. As Silvio Vega, another person implicated in the crime, declared, "Important persons of great influence" were involved in planning the assassination.[3] Undoubtedly, Somoza knew who killed his rival if he did not directly order the killing himself.

Opposition to Somoza escalated in response to this horrendous crime—horrendous, not because it was any more brutal than the thousands of other assassinations by Somoza of simple *campesinos* or well-known political opponents—but awesome in its political implications. The Democratic Union of Liberation (UDEL)—organized by Chamorro—immediately withdrew from the "national dialogue, saying that *somocismo* "has turned (once

16

again) to repression as the only means of keeping itself in power."[4] The Coordinating Committee, led by Archbishop Obando y Bravo, declared the Dialogue indefinitely suspended, for as the FSLN had prophesied only a day before Pedro Joaquin's death, "the dialogue is a lie against the people because it is slated to occur at the very moment the dictatorship is wounded unto death."[5] And so it was. Every opposition party closed ranks against the regime and called for Somoza's resignation: the Independent Liberal Party, the two factions of the Social Christian Party, the Socialist Party and even the Nicaraguan Conservative Party (PNC), which called for a joint strategy "in our final encounter against the tottering dictatorship."[6]

The most serious reaction came initially not only from the angry crowds and the politicians but from the upper class business community. They considered Pedro Joaquin the last presidential candidate who might lead a moderate political movement against the dictator. With Chamorro's death, the political climate in Nicaragua moved perilously close to anarchy, posing a direct threat to all business interests. Therefore, the business community decided to take the offensive; the Chamber of Commerce, the Chamber of Industries (CADIN), the Chamber of Builders, the Nicaraguan Institute of Development (INDE), the powerful High Council of Private Enterprise (COSEP), the Chamber of Customs Agents, and the Cotton Cooperative—the entire non-Somoza controlled bourgeoisie—created a "National Committee for a General Strike."[7] By January 22, this business work stoppage (paro empresarial) went into effect, closing down all business and industry in Nicaragua. The entire trade union movement supported the work halt, calling it a "General Strike for Justice."[8]

This unusual action of an upper-level capitalist class is not so hard to understand when one examines the degree to which Somoza and his friends dominated business and agricultural power in Nicaragua. Somoza's principal sin was that he had closed the capitalist class out of much of Nicaragua's economic potential as its "disloyal competitor."

To appreciate just how much wealth and power Somoza had amassed, here is a partial listing of his holdings:[9]

46 coffee farms	a fishing industry
7 sugar plantations	a meat packing firm
51 cattle farms	a milk processing company
400 tobacco farms	a cigar factory
1 gold mine	a shoe factory
3 radio stations	a transport line
2 airlines	a port
1 bank	tourist centers
1 newspaper	an insurance company

In addition, he owned industries producing oil, glass, textiles, matches, salt, ice, chemicals, jewelry, refined coffee, asbestos, cement, concrete, housing and aluminum products. Somoza and his cohorts owned approximately 50% of all arable land in Nicaragua, 40% of all industry and had liquid capital assets worth $400-600 million.[10]

Aside from wanting Somoza himself out of power, the Nicaraguan upper class was deeply troubled by the death of Pedro Joaquin Chamorro because it eliminated one of the few men who might rally the people around a liberal platform which could fill the political vacuum, effectively stopping the left. With Chamorro's death, this privileged economic class felt an urgency to remove Somoza from power so that some compromise between the business and

popular-left forces could be worked out. The next months were to be dominated by this hope.

The struggle between Chamorro and Somoza, however, had even deeper historical and psychological roots that impinged upon the political climate. Pedro Joaquin was not only Somoza's most outspoken critic; he was the dictator's symbolic opponent. Following his father's death in 1956 at the hand of Rigoberto López Pérez, Somoza had arrested Pedro Joaquin, along with hundreds of other suspects, and personally tortured him, even though he knew Chamorro had no connection with the assassination. The torture was a warning from Tacho Somoza, an act reminding "the opposition" of the vengeance that awaited all who openly resisted the dynasty. Furthermore, Chamorro was a direct political threat to the regime, whether as a liberal democrat (he described himself a Social-Christian), or as an idealistic Sandinista, which he was in the nationalistic sense. Chamorro had been a leader in reviving the spirit of Sandino. In 1965, he wrote:

> "As it is natural on the anniversary of an illustrious man (Sandino) to revive his memory, so too it is natural that those guilty of his death would try to kill him (again) or that those parties or servants who took his life, should now try to obliterate his memory."[11]

Since the spirit of Sandino was the only nationalist inspiration the people had against the Somozas, Pedro Joaquin, as the torch bearer of the spirit, was a direct symbolic threat to the dictatorship.

At the personal level, there was also a *macho* rivalry between the two men. Pedro Joaquin had been imprisoned many times, prohibited from writing or printing his newspaper, tortured and exiled. Each time it had been Tacho—his schoolmate opponent—who had personally executed the sentence and punishment. Given the outspokenness of Chamorro and the vindictive nature of Somoza, the two could not co-exist for long on the same turf. It was a struggle that could only end as it did, with the power of evil trampling down its arch enemy. And conversely, it was inevitable that from the tomb of that fallen martyr, the whole nation should rise up as a united people to carry out the society's judgment against this corrupt system.

In murdering Pedro Joaquin Chamorro, Somoza had overstepped a critical boundary and from that moment on, everything was downhill for the dictatorship. As one writer put it, "With this assassination, Somoza has committed (political) suicide."

BUSINESS WORK STOPPAGE & POPULAR UNREST

The leadership vacuum and potentially anarchic situation created by Chamorro's assassination prompted the business community to mobilize a "National Committee for a General Strike." The Committee consisted of leaders from the private business sector in a tactical alliance with the liberal and progressive parties. Together, these two sectors called upon all businessmen, employees, workers and students to join what was called a *strike*, but which in reality was a temporary "work stoppage" (*paro empresarial*) organized from the top down. This limited halt in business activities had a single, fundamental goal: to oust Somoza.

An unusual number of Nicaraguan and U.S. businesses and industries responded to this call: Soluble Coffee Expresso; the Nejapa, Montoya and El Punto y Camino commercial centers; ANDIVA automobile parts factory; the Medical Society of Managua; Tobacalera Nicaraguense; Kodak; National Cash Register; Coca Cola and Pepsi Cola. In Managua alone, some 200 business establishments—approximately 85% of all stores, centers, and industries—completely closed down. Supporting the businessmen were most labor unions, including the Carpenters & Finishers Union (SCAAS), the independent General Workers Central, the Nicaraguan Workers Central (CTN) and the Union of Popular Organizations (UNOP). Secondary support came from the opposition political parties: the Nicaraguan Conservative Party, the Social Christian Party, the Independent Party, the Independent Liberal Party, and others. Behind them followed the women's organization called AMPRONAC and church groups such as the "Christian Communities for Peace." Later, the National University students (CUUN), the banking sector, and various radio stations joined in the protest.

The work stoppage was "gathering greater strength with every passing moment."[1] Sometimes the strikers stood in traditional protest lines; more often they simply refused to

work and took voluntary vacations. In the face of this united opposition and social paralysis, there was little Somoza could do, except when the protestors took to the streets. Somoza had no intention of giving in to public pressure, but because of its magnitude he had to act very carefully. The dictator's strategy was to wait them out.

On January 27, the private sector issued its carefully worded and self-protective statement in support of the work stoppage.

In the face of the demands by the opposition parties that General Anastasio Somoza resign, and in view of the grave crisis the country is facing, we urge the President of the Republic in the spirit of disinterested patriotism, to consider this profound constitutional alternative which would lead the country towards a permanent climate of peace, based on justice, freedom, and democracy. [2]

Somoza could not tolerate such an open rejection, however diplomatically phrased. He replied in his typically adamant manner, declaring the country to be in a state of "public calamity"[3] and announcing his decision to reconstitute the National Committee of Emergency which had functioned following the crisis brought on by the 1972 earthquake. He called on all persons, businesses and industries to perform their civic duty by going back to work.

Such a response might weaken the resolve of the upper class but it could not contain the rising wrath of the popular sectors: now it was the people's turn. By January 28, protests in Matagalpa and Diriamba broke out, followed by huge gatherings of protestors in Managua, Masaya and San Carlos on the Costa Rican border. In the face of such public outbursts, Somoza could not be liberal. By January 30, the National Guard began moving, attacking women at a large peaceful demonstration at the United Nations building with tear gas, and brutalizing 3,000 students protesting at the National University. In León, Jinotega, Chinandega and Rivas, street barricades began to appear the following day. The Guard's level of violence escalated, with beatings, arrests, and shootings of dozens of protestors. The students tried to win some of the Guard over to their side with signs that read "Guards, control yourselves; don't kill your own people."[4] but their pleading was in vain. At night women took to the streets pounding on pots and pans, and young people set up barricades and burned tires on street corners during the day. The Guard responded by increasing its armed patrols in jeeps. These repressive patrol units, called BECATs, often shot people on sight or, as in the case of the extensive protests in the Managua *barrio* of OPEN-3, they physically beat protestors in broad daylight.

By February 3, it was clear that the work stoppage had failed to persuade Somoza to leave, and within the next few days, businesses began to re-open. The National Strike Committee declared an end to the closedown, but warned they were going to continue to press for independence in the judicial system, an apolitical National Guard, free trade unionism, and an end to Somoza's "disloyal competition."[5] The business sector was actually admitting that it had gone as far as it could by carrying out an 80% effective strike for two weeks across the nation. In effect, it had revealed to the Nicaraguan people the limits of its liberal pressures on the dictatorship.

While the bourgeois pressure on Somoza was declining,

Women in a peaceful protest outside Managua's U.N. building are tear gassed by the National Guard.

the initiative was being assumed by the FSLN and the popular forces. On February 2 and 3, the Sandinista Front (Insurrectional Tendency) had attacked and briefly taken over the cities of Grenada and Rivas in swift night raids, leaving behind the increasingly familiar red and black banners which read: "This city was occupied by the FSLN."[6] Somoza attempted a counter-propaganda campaign against the Sandinistas, saying that these attacks made a mockery of the "patriotic sadness" of the people following the death of Pedro Joaquin Chamorro. This cynical attitude only triggered more attacks by the FSLN. This time Peñas Blancas on the southern border and Nueva Segovia in the north were hit. Sabotage occurred as well in the port city of Corinto where huge bales of cotton were set on fire, while in Managua the antennae of TV station Channel 6 were destroyed.[7]

The Catholic church, meanwhile, continued its cautious anti-Somoza position while opposing the rising violence. It did allow its places of worship to be used as bases for clandestine news reports that came to be called "the press in the catacombs."[8] As the repression mounted, however, Archbishop Obando y Bravo began to qualify his non-violent position, stating that there were circumstances when armed resistance might be legitimate, as in the face of:

1. the existence of obvious and extreme injustice;
2. a proven failure of all forms of peaceful solution; and,
3. armed resistance which will produce fewer deaths than the existing injustices.[9]

Despite the growing resistance, Somoza refused to acknowledge defeat. By February 8, he declared that the Government had overcome the crisis brought on by the death of Pedro Joaquin and asserted: "As my father said: I will not leave nor will they make me go."[10] This continued obstinance before such widespread societal pressure only made the masses more aggressive. In Diriamba, those killed by the National Guard were carried through the streets in coffins draped in FSLN flags in open challenge to the dictatorship. In Monimbó (Masaya) 60 fused bombs were set off as that *barrio* was repeatedly barricaded. Similar protests broke out in Chinandega and Estelí, while in Masaya various buildings were burned down, including the homes of some of Somoza's spies.

The Guard's reaction to this resistance became comparably stronger and the number of shooting deaths rose sharply.

While the Chamber of Industries (INDE) could only protest, saying: "We declare our opposition and indignation at the rising level of violence by the Government,"[11] clearly, by mid-February the initiative had passed to the people.

MONIMBO: FLAME OF POPULAR RESISTANCE

The events of mid-to-late February 1978 in the indigenous, artisan, Indian community of Monimbó, located on the south edge of Masaya, signaled a turning point in the nature of resistance towards the dictatorship: a nationwide shift to all-out popular and armed rebellion.

The residents of Monimbó have a history of resistance to outside aggression dating to the interventionist actions of U.S. citizen William Walker in the late 1850's.[1] Instincts of preservation of their own people combined with their traditional hand craft skills equipped this tenacious, courageous sector of Nicaraguan society for rebellion.[2]

Along with cities and towns throughout Nicaragua,

20

Masaya rose up in indignation and anger at the assassination of Pedro Joaquin Chamorro. Public protest marches and religious services were held in various parts of town. The most intense struggle arose in Masaya among the thatched huts of the *barrio* Monimbó, where the Guard's repression provoked virtually every resident into explosive confrontation. Initiated by Monimbó's youth but rapidly gathering broader support, nightly harassment of known Somoza spies and supporters increased in tempo, leading to destruction and burnings of residences and cars belonging to *orejas*, spies of the Somoza interests.

By February 8, *La Prensa* reported that Masaya was practically under a state of siege. National Guardsmen forbade public meetings after 7:00 p.m., and forcibly broke up casual street corner conversations typical on the street of a small town in the evening. Even groups of children playing near their homes were forced to remain inside as the National Guard attempted to maintain control over the population.[3]

All residents of Masaya—professionals, students, workers, and farmers—joined Monimbó on February 11 to dedicate the Plaza in front of the *barrio's* San Sebastian Church to the memory of Pedro Joaquin Chamorro. The brief but emotional ceremony, in which representatives of UDEL warned the dictatorship of the rising wrath of its people, ended with unison cries of "Long Live Pedro Joaquin Chamorro!"[4]

The final straw for Monimbó came on February 20, the 40-day anniversary of the death of Chamorro. Approximately one thousand women, youth and children gathered in the San Sebastian Church for an afternoon mass to their hero. Upon leaving the church, the participants found the building surrounded by Guard patrol BECAT's who immediately opened fire, throwing more than fifteen tear gas bombs into the crowd of fleeing women and children. Many were wounded and required hospital treatment; 500 children attending classes in the nearby school center, Oratorio Festivo, also suffered from the effects of the bombs. Headlines of *La Prensa* the following day read "Monimbó is provoked, and responds," while photos depicted women running from the Guard, hands covering their burning faces.[5]

This brutal and indiscriminate attack on their women and children ignited the rebellion of the entire community. That night the angered population closed off the main street entrance with a large FSLN banner, set fire to the Guard vehicles and burned down the local Guadalajara theatre. The Guard retaliated with aerial bombardment at noon the following day, using tear gas on some of the most densely populated sectors of the *barrio*. Further incensed, the people set fire to houses of several known Somoza spies in Masaya, and began intense preparations for an all out rebellion.

On February 22, Monimbó's men, women, and children defiantly challenged Guard control of their *barrio*. Using the tools of their trade, the weapons available to the poor, and their artisan creativity, they confronted the Guardsmen. With sticks, clubs, machetes, and brick barricades, the very young and very old guarded strategic street entrances.

With eight 22-caliber rifles, four 38-caliber pistols, two grenades, and an arsenal of fused fireworks and home-made "contact bombs," the residents seized control of the *barrio*. Forcing the National Guard out of their streets and past the *barrio* entrance at the San Sebastian Church, the residents took possession of the plaza. Gathering with their home-made weapons raised victoriously, they shouted in unison, "Not even death will deter us!"[6] The Guard continued its brutal repression, combining aerial bombardment and ground attack, and refused Red Cross entry into the *barrio*, while it sought to re-take the area. *La Prensa* headlines of February 23 read: "Monimbo: the neighborhood struggles house by house."

With only crude and basic hand-made weapons, Monimbo held out against the sophisticated weaponry of the National Guard until February 27. To crush the rebellion, a Guard contingent of 600 soldiers directed by Tachito (the dictator's son) descended on Monimbó with tanks and machine guns in addition to aerial bombardment. At 11:00 that morning, planes and helicopters began flying low over the neighborhood; 45 minutes later bombing began. The fire was so massive that virtually the entire population was forced out of their homes and took refuge in the Red Cross center.[7] In its effort to re-gain control and crush any FSLN support, the National Guard left a bloody path of dead and wounded with as many as 200 young people unaccounted for.[8] Using heavy equipment from the Ministry of Public Works, the Guard "cleaned (out) the area of barricades and resistance."[9]

The Monimbó uprising and its toll of dead, wounded, and disappeared sent shock waves throughout the entire nation. *La Prensa* gave major, detailed, daily coverage to the developments, and the entire Nicaraguan population watched as this poor, indigenous sector of the society dared to openly challenge Somoza's massive power.

On March 2, 1978 the people of Monimbo published a dramatic open letter to Archbishop Obando y Bravo, pleading that he intervene on behalf of the hundreds from their *barrio* who had disappeared and were unaccounted for. The letter proclaimed to the entire nation that they had not been beaten down by Somoza and his National Guard. To the contrary, they were more determined than ever:

> *While Somoza remains as President, our people will rise up in protest to his cold-blooded crimes, robbery, corruption and the genocide we in Monimbó have experienced.... We in Monimbó want to clarify to the world that Somoza's delcarations are false. We are not influenced by communism, nor by any international ideology. We have our own Nicaraguan ideology: Somoza must go.*[10]

First in shock, then in admiration and pride, other cities and towns found in Monimbó's militancy an example of how to tell the world that Somoza must go. People in towns from the north to the south took up the challenge to make of every neighborhood, every village, every city and town *a Monimbó*.[11] The flame of resistance had indeed been handed over to the people and the FSLN.

Funeral procession in Masaya.

ORGANIZING THE CAMPESINOS: THE ATC

"...because only the workers and campesinos will go on until the end, only their organizing force will accomplish the triumph."
Augusto Cesar Sandino
Feb. 26, 1930

For the vast majority of Nicaragua's rural population, life under the Somoza dictatorship was a life of poverty, exploitation, and persecution. The 1950's introduced cotton production to Nicaragua, causing a massive redistribution of land away from individual farmers and into the hands of wealthy plantation owners. Even earlier than this, Somoza was also expanding his private agricultural holdings and forcing an increasing number of farmers either completely off the land or onto such small, marginally productive plots that they could not make a living on them. By 1976 Somoza was the largest landowner in the country.[1]

For the few individual farmers who managed to keep small plots of land as well as for plantation workers on the cotton, sugar and coffee plantations, social conditions were similar: chronic malnutrition, poor housing, lack of health care, illiteracy, seasonal employment, and repression by landowners who had the backing of local authorities and the National Guard. In contrast to most of Central and South American countries with long histories of rural movements, the National Guard's political repression and Somoza's private agro-business expansion effectively thwarted any efforts to organize *campesinos* until the 1970's.

The first concrete efforts to improve the living and working conditions of *campesinos* came from two religious groups, the Agrarian Promotion and Education Center (CEPA), and the "Delegates of the Word." CEPA was created by the Jesuit Order in 1969 and run under its auspicies for several years. It was a rural pastoral program which trained leaders in the theory and practice of organizing "grassroots communities."[2] During the period of 1970-76, under constant threat of repression and frequent accusation of subversive activity, CEPA gave seminars to priests, plantation workers, and other people who worked in the departments of Carazo and Masaya, primarily on coffee plantations. These seminars sought to integrate biblical reflection and technical agricultural training, particularly the introduction of intermediate technology. CEPA published a small cartoon-form pamphlet, *Cristo, Campesino*, which offered basic theological-political messages such as "You have a right to land."

Many of the participants in CEPA's seminars were part of another Catholic movement, "Delegates of the Word," who were also working to improve peasant conditions throughout the country. In line with the sweeping reforms outlined for the Catholic Church at the 1968 Medellin Conference of Latin American Biships, Nicaragua's Catholic hierarchy sought ways to bring the church to its own poor. Lacking a reserve of priests to call on for this task, the church offered basic training to lay people, who returned to their own communities with their social justice-oriented gospel message. On coffee plantations in the departments of Carazo and Masaya, the "Delegates" and plantation workers had been demanding basic health care services, drinking water, livable salaries, and year-round employment.[3]

As a result of CEPA's reflection/training seminars and the social work done by such individuals as the "Delegates," plantation workers in Carazo and Masaya formed Committees of Agricultural Workers whose primary goal was to collectively demand improvements in living conditions. These Committees grew in number and spread to other plantations through the Carazo and Masaya region. The wealthy landowners and National Guard retaliated, labelling any peasant organizing subversive. Peasants were subjected to beatings, torture, murder, and imprisonment. Because Sandino's army was peasant-based and the FSLN had its operating base in the countryside, peasants were continually suspect of being Sandinistas or their supporters. When accused (regardless of proof) they were arrested, or "disappeared" permanently.

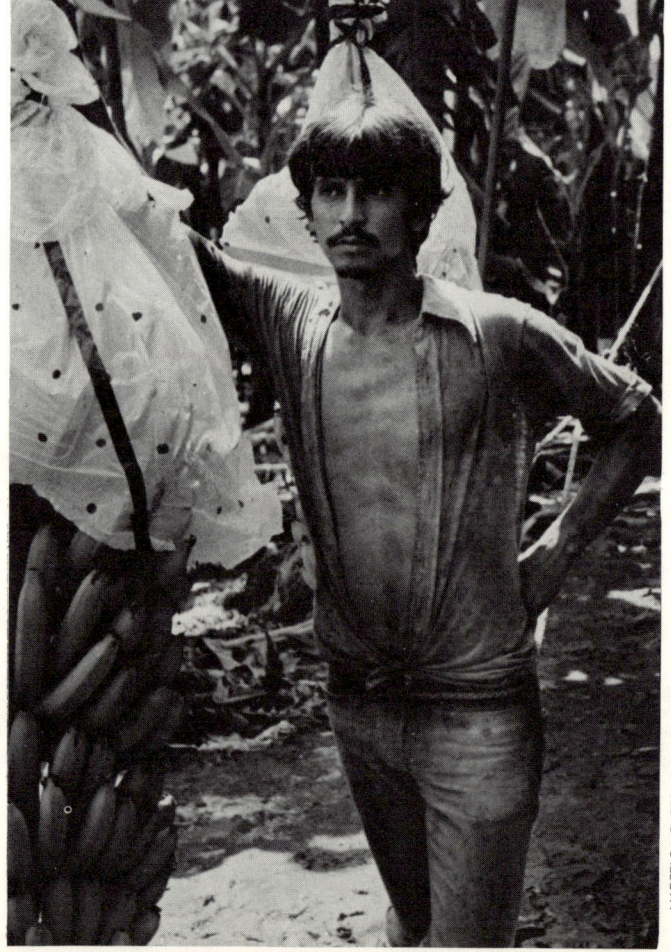

Banana plantation worker in the Chinandega region.

Nicaragua's landless peasantry suffered years of poverty and repression under the dictatorship.

This intense peasant repression actually backfired on Somoza. Thousands of peasants had already labelled Somoza the "enemy" because of his take-overs of their land. These landless peasants wanted their land, and they wanted to get even with Somoza. When they found their comrades and families bearing the brunt of the National Guard's systematic "clean-up," they escalated their organizing. Committees of Agricultural Workers spread from the pacific region's coffee plantations to cotton and sugar plantations. By late 1977, the northern Pacific zone was the most militant sector of the population.[4]

The FSLN's involvement in this process of *campesino* organizing first began in 1975 (following the TP-GPP tendency split) when the TP made the decision to begin working with peasants. However, this was a slow process. At that time the National Guard's repression held peasants in such a state of terror that they would have nothing to do with the Sandinista Front. Nevertheless, as the Committees of Agricultural Workers spread throughout the Pacific region, the FSLN increased its contacts and influence.

In 1977, the Sandinistas formed an Association of Rural Workers (ATC) which united all the Committees in the Departments of Carazo, Masaya, León, Chinandega, and Managua. The ATC's ultimate purpose was to unite all *campesinos* around demands for improved living conditions, year-round employment, and an end to political repression for the entire agricultural working class. The National Guard's continued crackdown on the peasant population—resulting in hundreds of disappeared, imprisoned, tortured or murdered—fueled their rising political consciousness. Some of the Delegates and other leaders became FSLN sympathizers, and the Committees become more accessible to the FSLN:

Neither the struggle to organize as groups on plantations nor the struggle in the fields offered us great possibilities for throwing off the exploiters who had robbed us for so long. It became clear to us that we needed to organize as a social class, organize on every plantation where the salaries were so poor, where the struggle was direct and focused. Where the politi-

cal development was broadest among the plantation and farm workers, this was where we united. [5]

More and more peasants joined the struggle at the organizational level during 1977, as they began to see the link between their struggle in the countryside and the struggle against the dictatorship. The ATC had spread to the northernmost Pacific agricultural zones and as far south as the Department of Rivas.[6]

During the fall of 1977, the ATC held public protest rallies and religious services to denounce the disappearances of many of their comrades in the north. In October public demands were made on sugar cane and coffee plantations. Members of the ATC went to Managua in December and joined the civil protests denouncing the dictatorship which were organized in several *barrios*. In each instance, the Guard attacked furiously with tear gas, beatings, and often with open machine gun fire. Following the January 1978 assassination of Chamorro and the work stoppage, ATC members led the blocking of main roads and highways, virtually paralyzing the National Guard. They also cut communication lines in many rural areas.

By March 1978 the ATC was organized with departmental representatives coordinating their work between zones. Sub-committees were set up to coordinate security and defense, finances, political education, and public information. Committees in the regions of Tonala, Sirama, Villa Salvadorita, San José del Obraje, and others began making demands that farms in their regions be turned over to worker control. Urban workers—originally from the countryside but now working in small factories, public transportation and small stores—had also joined the ATC. In April the first issue of a *campesino* newsletter, *El Machete*, was published and distributed nationwide, facilitating the political consciousness and visibility of the ATC.

On April 9, 1978, the ATC initiated a march and hunger strike in Diriamba, in the Department of Masaya. To call national attention to the starvation of the peasant population, 1,200 ATC members and supporters came onto Diriamba's streets protesting the plight of their comrades and families. Anticipating the event, EEBI forces of the National Guard had been harassing and terrorizing members of the ATC on their plantations for a week preceeding

REVOLUTION

The mountain began
greening with the
intensity of our hope.

A spontaneous poem
began to arise
in the throats of birds
until it became a fullness.

A light from the sky
cradled the ideals of our people
and turned night into day.

Now the oppressor lays asleep forever:
In the morning, the mountain became green
with the intensity of our hope.

The people sang
and called out to one another.

Justice wore a white veil
with a bunch of red roses in her hands.

A campesino march in the Chinandega area.

the march, and had captured several key leaders the night of April 8. On the morning of April 9, the National Guard guarded every entrance to Diriamba, and completely occupied the intersection from which the march was to begin. When the ATC shifted its mobilization two blocks away from the original site, they were immediately confronted by Guardsmen who attempted to disperse them with

tear gas bombs. Diriamba's residents opened their doors to the marchers and offered pans of water to relieve their burning faces. Unable to deter them, the Guard opened fire and "spewed a flood of bullets on the marching participants...in the ATC's first baptism of blood."[7]

While the Guard frustrated the march itself, they could not prevent the news of it from spreading quickly throughout the country. The repression of the march prompted a barrage of hunger strikes instantaneously taken up by women from AMPRONAC, secondary students, and university opposition groups. From Diriamba these hunger strikes spread both North and South as the entire population expressed its solidarity with the ATC and its *campesino* members.

The hunger march and resulting hunger strike forced a crucial change in the ATC: the peasants were now ready to challenge Somoza's power.[8] "The grassroots committees of the ATC thus became committees in support of all-out war (against the dictatorship) and carried out their political line in conjunction with the FSLN. During May, June, July and August, hundreds from the ATC armed and organized themselves in popular militias,[9] while others continued their work on plantations and farms. Their homes became virtual Sandinista strongholds and their goal was one and the same with the FSLN: "Death to the dictatorship; Death to Somocismo."[10]

STUDENT MOBILIZATION AGAINST THE DICTATORSHIP

"Our army of workers and campesinos wants to fraternize with the students, because we understand that it is from among this army and from them that we will discover those who with new orientations will make of our land a country of light."
                            Augusto Cesar Sandino

The national student movement against the dictatorship was consolidated by April 1978. This was the fruit of intermittent but rising student rebelliousness during the 1975-77 state of siege period. During these years, protests were led primarily by high school students in the Association of Secondary Students (AES) and the Secondary Student Movement (MES), reflecting the GPP and TP tendencies, respectively. These organizations mobilized student groups under the slogan, "Don't allow a single act

of repression or a single crime by the dictatorship to go by without denouncing it everywhere."[1]

This gradually-building student movement was centered in the Departments of Managua and Carazo, and to a lesser degree in León, Chinandega and Estelí. In its earlier period, the movement was weakly organized and suffered, in part, from the FSLN divisions which became increasingly public during 1976 and 1977. From 1977 on, the secondary students from the Cristobal Colón and Andrés Bello schools in Managua gradually established links with the students at the Universidad Centroamericana (UCA), also in the capital. Their joint efforts grew until, by the end of 1977, rallies sometimes numbered as many as 2,000 students. During that year, the growing repression of the National Guard forced the students into using specialized techniques of resistance: pickets in front of schools, street bonfires, "lightning meetings,"[2] and spray painting of political slogans at night.

The first successful political action led by students came in the Summer of 1977, when the government raised bus fares by 40 *centavos* (5 cents) per ride. This decision created great personal hardship on the poor and produced nationwide indignation. Students decided to lead the protests against the fare hike. In order to focus public anger, students let air out of tires, broke bus windows, and set wooden boards filled with nails on streets and highways. Such tactics crippled bus transportation which, in turn, hurt commercial business. This campaign brought students off campus and into the streets, forcing them to mix with the common people, deepening their understanding of the economic struggle of the masses.

In December 1977, student protests responded to more serious political issues: increased political prisoners and the repression of *campesinos*. As a result of the FSLN's October attacks, the National Guard stepped up its presence in urban areas as well as in the countryside. The students responded with protest marches at which they carried placards reading: "Where are our *campesino* brothers and sisters?" and "Christmas 77 without political prisoners!"[3]

Student slogan sprayed on a city wall in Leon: "Socialism is the only system capable of guaranteeing the real development of Nicaragua. Unity Among Student Combatants."

Given the extreme social conditions at this time, acts of protest against human rights violations quickly turned political. Students not only protested in the streets; they began to take over churches and schools which they held in some cases for days. As a consequence, National Guard repression increased, forcing the students to learn how to defend themselves against tear gas attacks, prepare supply caches before taking over buildings, set up communications systems, and defend themselves behind street barricades.

The assassination of Pedro Joaquin Chamorro in January 1978 became the next motivation for increased student resistance. The four weeks of struggle during the previous December had given the students the preparation they needed to become leaders in the post-assassination events. During January and February, three other pro-Sandinista organizations became politically active: the Revolutionary Student Front (FER), the Nicaraguan Revolutionary Youth (JRN) and the University Center for Popular Solidarity (CUSOP). Because the post-Chamorro funeral period was also the time of the work stoppage, many workers were at home and students developed contacts with trade unions and individual factory committees; for the first time, students and workers marched together in political protests. The rising political nature of these protests forced the National Guard to adopt new tactics such as increased use of the "Special Brigades Against Terrorist Acts" (BECATs). These armed teams of Guardsmen, usually travelling four in a jeep, arrested and shot students and young people on sight. In turn, the students responded with ever more aggressive counter-tactics.

This rising resistance was only a prelude to the explosive period of April 6 to May 9. During these 33 days of continuous struggle, students and young people in general became the vanguard of the civilian uprisings in many cities. This period of organized rebellion started around the end of March 1978 when Albertina Serrano, a widow, began a hunger strike to protest the solitary confinement of her son, Marcio Jaén, and that of FSLN founder Tomás Borge. This hunger strike was first supported by AMPRONAC and then by the students at the National Institute of Masaya (INMA). In addition to demanding freedom for Jaén and Borge, the INMA students insisted that the faculty expel all teachers who were serving as Somoza's spies, and denounced the National Guard's widespread distribution of marihuana and other drugs to students in order to weaken their resistance and organizing capabilities.

On April 6, the most massive and prolonged student strike in the history of Nicaragua began. By April 8, some 20 schools and institutes throughout the country had been taken over. This produced an open struggle between students and the Guard, with the soldiers retaking several educational centers and converting them into military headquarters. Within a few days, 38 persons had joined Albertina Serrano's fast. The example of the students in the Carazo area spread to other cities. They developed close unity with trusted professors, mobilized their parents and the parent-student organization "Family Parents," and became the leading vanguard of the popular struggle in their cities. Progressive students also converted many previously traditional and conservative Catholic schools into militant anti-Somoza centers.

Before the national strike was over, more than 60,000 students had become directly involved and had successfully crippled the entire educational system. Somoza had to use moderation with the student uprising because of the positive image the students had with the general population and because of their links with the middle and upper classes. Nevertheless, in a number of cities (like Diriamba, Jinotega and Estelí) the National Guard was ruthless, using tear gas, mustard gas,[4] and indiscriminate shooting to break up pickets and drive students out of buildings. Hundreds of students were arrested, wounded or killed.

Despite the growing aggressiveness of the Guard, the students did not lose their resolve following the end of the strike. On July 9, students protested against the *Somocista* representative in the Ministry of Public Relations, Elena de Porra. In that protest, four students were killed. During a massive funeral procession held for the fallen students, whose caskets were draped with FSLN flags, over 10,000 *cordobas* were collected and used to buy arms for the next encounter.

Exemplary of these student struggles is a May 1978 account of events in Estelí:

A student center in Estelí had been taken over by young people (including children 6-10 years of age). These youngsters were violently forced out of the buildings and an unimaginable number were beaten, or shot. This act moved the citizens of Estelí to realize they must respond in like manner. They destroyed the property and houses of Somoza officials in retaliation. Recovery of arms became commonplace.[5] One military armory was totally emptied of arms as the people prepared to follow the insurrectional leadership of the FSLN vanguard. All these events helped create the material conditions for the moment when the entire nation would initiate its final struggle for liberation."[6]

Thus the student strike of April and May and student leadership represented the single most important vanguard of the urban struggle. More than any other sector, it was the students who built the momentum which culminated in the September insurrection.

THE ROLE OF WOMEN IN THE REVOLUTION: AMPRONAC

**You are pretty in your fashionable dress
on Central Avenue
but you are prettier still at the training camp
with your uniform and your rifle.
Bosco Centeno**

The early development of the women's movement in opposition to the Somoza dictatorship corresponded to the rapidly rising social discontent which developed in the 1970's among Nicaragua's middle and upper classes. For women within these classes, this discontent was exacerbated by their own rising consciousness about women's rights. The repression of the Somoza regime radicalized the female bourgeosie's traditionally-held elitist, maternalistic, almost missionary attitude towards the poor.

During the 1970's, an increasing number of Nicaraguan women had become their families' principal wage earner. This, along with the injustices of lower wages, long working hours, and less upward job mobility than men, brought the traditional societal exploitation of women to a boiling point. Women began to demand decent wages, better housing, health care, education for their children, and equal employment opportunities at the very time when the Somoza system was least able to respond.

Following the 1972 earthquake and during the state of siege, women reacted to the increasingly repressive political situation and violence of Somoza's National Guard. They organized themselves to address the injustices suffered by the poorer majority as symptomatic of the overall discrimination against women. The Association of Nicaraguan Women Confronting the National Problem (AMPRONAC), began denouncing the human rights violations which symbolized the many problems confronting the nation. AMPRONAC encouraged Nicaraguan women to become more aware of their own social reality, to utilize and share their knowledge and resources with one another, and to defend their right as Nicaraguan women.[1] AMPRONAC envisioned a women's organization which would transcend the class structures of society, uniting all women in both affirming female rights and denouncing human rights violations. At a gathering of approximately 70 women in Managua on September 29, 1977, AMPRONAC became an official organization under the leadership of Lea Guido de López, Clariza Alvarez Sacasa, Tere Cardenal de Delgadillo, and Carmen de Brenes.[2]

Although small in number, from its inception AMPRONAC was a very visible organization. As a human rights group, its primary activities centered on investigating and denouncing the disappearance and imprisonment of women

Women from Monimbo; many women who joined the ranks of the FSLN were also members of AMPRONAC. Women would constitute upward of 30% of the FSLN's combatants by the final insurrection.

and children. As it initiated a massive educational effort, cities across the country began seeing AMPRONAC posters proclaiming a National Campaign Defending Citizen's Rights. Advocating "Nicaraguans, know your rights," the posters illustrated constitutional prohibitions against being detained without legal order for arrest, remaining in jail more than 24 hours without charge, the obligation of the State to respect the privacy of the home, and the right to publicly express one's personal opinion.[3]

Combined with this educational campaign, AMPRONAC began publishing in *La Prensa* documentation on those who had suffered as victims of the state of siege and on other human rights violations. AMPRONAC called for women and the entire Nicaraguan population to protest the government's flagrant abuses of these rights. It also published a long list of persons who had disappeared. *La Prensa* quoted the AMPRONAC directorate:

> *"As Nicaraguan women and citizens conscious of our constitutional rights and duties, we feel obliged to denounce the situation of terror under which the Nicaraguan people live."*[4]

On November 19, 1977 AMPRONAC joined a nationally publicized religious service held at the Catholic church in Las Palmas, Managua, where more than 1,000 persons gathered under the theme, "Where are our *campesino* brothers and sisters?" During this assembly—one of the largest during the state of siege—the Catholic Capuchin Fathers presented documents detailing the cases of 350 *campesinos* and young people from rural zones in the Atlantic coast region, while AMPRONAC brought forth relatives of some of the disappeared to make public testimonies.

With the specific short-term goal of expanding their membership to encompass the majority of Nicaraguan women, AMPRONAC began organizing chapters in other cities. Thus, during November and December 1977, AMPRONAC expanded its organizational base, holding assemblies around the country to make public the growing number of cases of imprisonment, torture, and death suffered by the peasant population at the hands of the National Guard. Assemblies were held in León and Matagalpa,[5] and in December AMPRONAC sent observers to the coordinators' meeting in preparation for the National Dialogue.[6]

The rapid chain of events set off by the January 1978 assassination of Pedro Joaquin Chamorro moved AMPRONAC one step closer to the popular struggle. On January 26, twelve women from the Atlantic coast occupied the United Nations' offices in Managua, representing the desperate families of disappeared persons. During this two-week takeover, AMPRONAC publically came to their support and called other popular organizations to follow suit. Daily support pickets were organized by AMPRONAC. These culminated on January 30 with a picket of more than 100 women. After three hours of peaceful protest in the patio of the United Nations building, the women were suddenly confronted by the National Guard. Under the direction of Chief of Police, Alesio Gutierrez, they were violently forced off the premises with tear gas and physical abuse.[7]

This experience of direct abuse by the Guard radicalized the leaders of AMPRONAC and contributed to the organization's broadened base of support. Many working class and peasant women, also politicized because of National Guard violence, joined AMPRONAC. Thus, by February, AMPRONAC concentrated its energies on organizing women into an opposition force openly challenging the Somoza regime.[8] By March, AMPRONAC's membership was estimated at more than 1,000 women, representing chapters in the departments of Managua, Carazo, Chinandega, León, and Granada.[9]

On March 8, 1978, AMPRONAC initiated International Mothers Week by calling all Nicaraguan women to join the struggle for a free country, stating that Nicaragua could not legitimately speak of "popular" resistance without including the large female population.[10] That week, masses were celebrated in churches across the country in memory of the many Nicaraguan mothers who had died at the hands of the National Guard. The León chapter held a radio marathon in cooperation with the Central University to collect medicines and money for Monimbó.[11] The chapters of Diriamba and Jinotepe published in *La Prensa* an open letter to the Spanish Embassy announcing the discovery of unexploded bombs in their Department of Carazo labelled "made in Spain."[12]

Early April brought this radicalization process of AMPRONAC to its peak. The Association of Rural Workers (ATC) initiated a massive hunger march in Diriamba to bring to national attention the plight of the *campesinos* in Carazo. The march was particularly important because only a few days earlier, the Government had been extolling its concern for the rural situation in Nicaragua. Because the march openly challenged Somoza's claim, the National Guard attacked the *campesinos* and their supporters, including women, and one of AMPRONAC's members was killed. AMPRONAC was outraged. As they described it in a subsequent report:

"For AMPRONAC this was an extremely important step in the development of our commitment to the struggle and its consequences.... It reaffirmed our reputation as an Association of Women and significantly increased the legitimacy of our role in the popular struggle."[13]

AMPRONAC immediately endorsed the *campesino* action, joining hunger strikes which spontaneously erupted across the country. When Somoza publicly stated, "We are very concerned for the health and development of our Nicaraguan workers and farmers," AMPRONAC demanded: "Do you call the bloody repression of all their efforts to obtain better living conditions a form of encouragement for these oppressed people?"[14]

By joining and extending the ATC-initiated hunger strikes, AMPRONAC completed a process of linking women's and human rights issues with popular opposition to the dictatorship. Its press conferences held in Chinandega, Diriamba, Boaco, and Jinotepe,[15] giving public confirmation of the plight of the peasants, further linked the organization to this exploited class. Urban and rural sectors had joined forces to bring down the dictatorship.

"Revolutionary Women—Free, Honest, Hardworking—To The Front."

THE CONSOLIDATION OF POPULAR FORCES: THE MPU

By July 1978, most of the popular forces had joined a single bloc called the United People's Movement (MPU). The MPU was a "political alliance of popular progressive forces"[1] including women, students, workers, *campesinos*, trade unions, political parties and revolutionary organizations. Months of meetings and discussion were required to produce this structural unity, and the MPU did not become an effective working unit until the September uprisings.

The origins of the MPU go back to the formation of the Permanent Commission for Human Rights (CPDH), founded on October 26, 1977.[2] While human rights was the initial motivating issue, "active unity" only emerged in December when women (AMPRONAC) and students (MES) joined forces around the repression of *campesinos*. In January and February 1978, this cooperative effort took a quantitative leap forward during the post-Chamorro protests. But it wasn't until March 29, around the issue of Marcelo Jaén's and Tomás Borge's imprisonment, that human rights concerns produced what has been called a "united political struggle of the masses against *somocismo*."[3]

At that time, the FSLN recognized the need for a broad-based organization, so during April and May groups directly linked to the Sandinista Front and independent but sympathetic sectors held a series of meetings aimed at "a dialogue towards unity."[4] The unification process was slowed by the constant threat of repression by the regime. Nevertheless, by June for the first time all three FSLN tendencies were represented in these discussions.[5] The only point of disagreement in these meetings was about whether such an organization should be a political party or a mass-based popular organization.

In July 1978, the group of "The Twelve,"[6] twelve individuals representing the progressive-liberal sector of Nicaragua's upper middle class, returned from exile in Costa Rica. Somoza decided, under pressure from the United States government, to allow the group temporary freedom to express its views, his last such gesture of freedom toward the "legal opposition."[7]

The arrival of "The Twelve" produced a massive outpouring in Managua, both at the airport and during the group's triumphal drive through the city. Aided by the media—including the international press—the group publically invoked the image of Sandino and declared themselves to be Sandinistas.[8] "The Twelve" recognized the legitimate role of the FSLN, although its contacts and sympathies were mainly with the most conciliatory sector, the *Tercerista* tendency. This endorsement made the entire FSLN more acceptable to many who still had their doubts. This massive turnout, however, should not be equated with effective organization. The MPU was playing the crucial

Members of The Twelve are welcomed by thousands of Nicaraguans from their exile in Costa Rica, July 1978.

SUSAN MEISELAS/MAGNUM

32

organizing role at this moment in Nicaragua's history.

In this context, on July 17, twenty-two organizations formally united into a single coalition of popular forces. They defined the three principle objectives of the MPU:

1. To mobilize the people for the popular overthrow of the Somoza dictatorship;
2. To expand the organization and to unify broad popular sectors; and
3. To advance the development of a unitary process between the revolutionary forces.[9]

The MPU called upon the Nicaraguan masses, and indeed upon all popular sectors and organizations,

"to strengthen the struggle against somocismo by closing ranks within the MPU—the great front of popular struggle that represents the highest interests of this process and which constitutes for the masses the fullest guarantee for the independence of all classes and mass parties and their combative organizations."[10]

It is important to list the constituent organizations of the MPU in order to appreciate the breadth of the movement and its popular makeup, an aspect completely lacking among the traditional parties (liberal or conservative) and the conciliatory Broad Opposition Front (FAO). The following organizations signed as founders of the MPU on July 17, 1978:

- Committee of Struggle for Union Freedom (CLLS)
- Workers Union, University Ruben Dario (STRURD)
- General Workers Confederation, Independent (CGT Independiente)
- Action & Unity Union Federation (CAUS)
- National Union of Employees (UNE)
- Working People (PT)
- Organization of Democratic Women of Nicaragua (OMDN)

- Nicaraguan Revolutionary Youth (JRN)
- Nicaraguan Socialist Party (PSN)
- Communist Party of Nicaragua (PC de N)
- Committee of Mothers & Families of Political Prisoners
- Association of Democratic Lawyers of Nicaragua (AADN)
- Federation of Youth Movements of Nicaragua (FMJM)
- Union of Progressive Intellectuals and Artists of Central America (UIAPCA)
- Revolutionary Student Front, Marxist-Leninist (FER M-L)
- Revolutionary Student Front (FER)
- Nicaraguan Socialist Youth (JSN)
- University Center of the National University (CUUN)
- Secondary Students Association (MES)
- Student Center of the Politechnic University (CEUPOLI)
- Revolutionary Workers Movement (MORE)
- Secondary Student Association (AES)[11]

Soon after MPU's official beginning, other prestigious organizations like the national women's group, AMPRONAC, also joined.

On July 26, the MPU made their coalition public at a meeting held in Managua's National University, where some 2,000 students, workers and professors gathered to outline their objectives. The MPU was more than a mass organization opposed to Somoza; it had a definite program that clearly outlined elements of an alternative political platform. In time the points delineated in July became the basis for the program of the future Government of National Reconstruction, including:

1. A democratic government, representative of the forces which struggle in a committed manner for the overthrow of the military Somoza dictatorship.
2. Transformation of the National Guard into an army that will guarantee the democratic accomplishments of the working class and the eradication of the dictatorship.
3. Application of justice to those responsible for the crimes committed against the people.
4. Confiscation of all holdings fraudulently accumulated or usurped by *somocismo*.
5. Fight for full economic and political independence, and rejection of every attempt at foreign intervention into the internal affairs of the country.
6. Agrarian reform that guarantees productive lands, technical assistance and financing for poor *campesino* families.
7. Assurance of broad political and trade union organizations for the workers.
8. Promotion of revolutionary measures in the legal and institutional order that will assure the social rights of the worker in terms of salary, health, housing and education; and to eradicate the miserable conditions, education and culture for working families.[12]

Although the MPU had decided it should be primarily a mass-based coalition, by late July it had also become, in effect, a progressive pre-party which challenged the liberal FAO. This intent was made clear at the July 26 meeting when a spokesperson for the MPU, Jaime Rivera, predicted an important development:

While I cannot respond concretely about the possible union with the Broad Opposition Front and UDEL— because that will be considered in future discussions— I suppose that we are moving towards national unity in order to install a popular, democratic and progressive government which will allow the Nicaraguan people to move forward to the point where we can bring about a truly just social and political change in Nicaragua.[13]

The open combative challenge to the Somoza regime during the next two months, however, moved the political climate forward much more rapidly than anyone had anticipated. This radical development thrust the business-oriented FAO into a conciliatory role which would soon exclude any projected unity with the MPU.

ATTACK ON THE NATIONAL PALACE

"I am not willing to give up my arms even though all the others do so. I would rather die with the few who accompany me because it is better for us to die as rebels than to live as slaves."

Augusto Cesar Sandino
May 12, 1927

The FSLN rationale for attacking the National Palace in Managua (Nicaragua's Congress) stemmed from two factors: one, a new U.S. tactic; the other, a long-standing Nicaraguan reality. The U.S. government had apparently adjusted its previous policy of pressuring Somoza on human rights. In July Jimmy Carter had sent Somoza a personal letter congratulating him on his "concern to improve human rights in Nicaragua." This suggested to the left forces that the United States had decided to help Somoza remain in power until 1981. The totally unrepresentative Congress—dominated by Somoza's own Liberal Party—was the only facade of democracy left to the regime to justify itself before the international community. Yet, the National Palace was the place where each day ever more onerous laws were being passed, legitimizing the dictator's control over and exploitation of the society.

The plan of attack, as Gabriel García Márquez described it, seemed "an overly simplistic madness."[1] With only 25 guerillas, the Sandinista Front intended to take over the National Palace and hold 67 members of the Chamber of Deputies and 2,500 bureaucrats until Somoza met the demands of the FSLN. The plan was originally conceived by the veteran leader, Edén Pastora, who was selected to lead the operation under the title Commander Zero. Despite the audacity of the strategy, the Sandinista High Command considered the plan a stroke of "crazy genius" with tremendous potential. The goals of freeing key political prisoners and giving broad publicity to the FSLN were fulfilled beyond their most optimistic expectations.

On August 22 at 12:30 p.m., just after the Chamber of Deputies had opened its midday session, two Ford trucks painted olive green, covered with military tarpaulins, pulled up in front of two lateral entrances to the Palace guarded by armed security forces. They were loaded with guerillas in full combat dress identical to National Guard uniforms. Commander Zero and his adjudants, Hugo Torres Jimenez, Commander One—who had taken part in the 1974 attack on the Castillo residence—and Dora María Telléz, Commander Two, quickly jumped out of the trucks. The three leaders were followed by their carefully trained cadre carrying Uzi sub-machine guns and G3, M3, M2 and Garand rifles. Acting boldly, as if they were a special security guard contingent of the dictator, they ordered the security police to get back, because "The Chief is coming!" The police were quickly disarmed and the Sandinistas were inside.

Instantly, the FSLN attack force ran through the corridors of the Palace, stationing themselves at pre-designated key locations. One group of palace guards opened fire on the guerillas who retaliated, killing three guards plus the captain of the security force. Next, the commanders rushed to the main Chamber, shouting, "The Guard: everyone on the floor.!" The congressmen complied and lay face down, believing that this was a *coup d'etat* by a segment of the National Guard against Somoza, a possibility the Nicaraguan bourgeosie had long since anticipated. Commander One entered the rear of the so-called "Blue Room" and leapt over the prostrated bodies of congressmen just as Zero reached the presidential table from the other end. Outside the Chamber, a brief exchange of shots rang out. As a group of palace guards entered the Chamber and shot at the guerillas, Zero threw a hand grenade into their midst which instantly killed them, completing the takeover. The whole operation, which had taken six months to organize, was over in three minutes.

Somoza heard the news a few moments later and ordered the National Guard to surround the Palace and fire on the building indiscriminately, without interruption. Despite their counter offensive, the Guard could not re-take the building because of heavy firepower from the FSLN. Twenty minutes later, the dictator received a phone call from his cousin, Luis Palláis, from within the Palace and Somoza called off the barrage. The dictator was soon informed of the Sandinista Front's request that Archbishop Miguel Obando y Bravo and the bishops of Leon and Granada act as intermediaries (as Obando had done in 1974) and that they contact the ambassadors of Costa Rica and Panama, asking them to inform the international community of the takeover. The FSLN then revealed its demands: the National Guard must retreat to a distance of 300 meters from the Palace; the Government must donate $10 million to the Sandinista Front; freedom must be granted to specified political prisoners, and the FSLN attackers must be transported out of Nicaragua without challenge. Somoza stalled. The next

Dora Maria Tellez

Eden Pastora. Victory greetings at the airport.

morning he made his counter-demand: remove all women, children and wounded before negotiations could continue—something the FSLN had already accomplished through the Red Cross during the night.

The "life insurance" of the guerillas was with them there in the Palace: the bulk of the leadership of Somoza's Liberal Party; a number of his close associates and relatives; and members of the loyal opposition of Nicaragua's bourgeoisie, the Conservative Party. Somoza realized his disadvantage; only time might provide a way to free his captive allies. Meanwhile, the Sandinistas recognized that time was against them because of their limited energy, short supply of ammunition, and lack of food and water. They gave Somoza an ultimatum: a definite answer and action within 24 hours or they would begin to execute their prisoners. Publicly, Somoza continued to stall, but behind the scenes he was already beginning to meet the Sandinista's demands as political prisoners in distant dungeons were being aroused and brought to the capital. At the same time, Carlos Andrés Pérez, the President of Venezuela, and General Omar Torrijos of Panama added pressure on Somoza and promised their assistance in complying with the FSLN demands. Both offered aircraft to fly the attackers and political prisoners out of Nicaragua.

With pressure mounting within the Palace, on August 24, after 45 hours without sleep, the Sandinista guerrillas, five negotiators and four prisoners left the Congress in buses headed for the airport. The prisoners selected were the most important ones: Luis Palláis, first cousin of the dictator, José Somoza Abrego, son of Anastasio's half-brother; José Antonio Mora and Eduardo Chamorro, of the ruling parties. At the same hour, 60 political prisoners were already aboard two aircraft flying to Panama. The FSLN had ordered that no National Guard were to be seen on the way to the airport. On the other hand, the FSLN could do nothing about the huge crowds that gathered along the highway to offer the heroes their uncontrollable ovation. As Commander One said in good humor but ironically: "You see, this is the only thing you can't buy with silver."[2]

The attack on the National Palace had previously been discussed by all three tendencies of the FSLN, and somewhat reluctantly the GPP and Proletarian sectors had agreed to participate. Apparently communications broke down or were delayed and the action was, in fact, executed solely by the Insurrectionalists. The impact of the attack, however, affected all three factions positively and brought them closer together, by 1) freeing political prisoners from all three tendencies; 2) showing the two more skeptical factions the value of this form of struggle; and 3) impressing the world community with the potential of the FSLN.

The success of the attack had a tremendous impact on the Nicaraguan people and on the international community which gave the event unusual publicity. It not only signified humiliation for Somoza, but proved the effectiveness of guerilla tactics against the National Guard. The successful operation helped many Nicaraguans accept the fact that the FSLN might defeat Somoza and become the new government. At the same time, the attack deeply troubled the Nicaraguan bourgeoisie, forcing them to seek a more moderate solution to Nicaragua's mounting crisis.

THE SEPTEMBER INSURRECTION OF 1978

"Red and black are the colors lighting our banner, symbolizing with these colors, 'Liberty or Death', that is to say, the firm proposition of being 'Free, Sovereign and Independent'."
Augusto Cesar Sandino
Oct. 26, 1930

"Somoza bricks," the main street construction material in the country.

Immediately after the FSLN successfully seized the National Palace on August 25, 1978 the Broad Opposition Front (FAO) initiated its second attempt at a national work stoppage. As in the days following the death of Pedro Joaquin Chamorro, the FAO's business constituency again felt the climate was ripe for pressuring Somoza to leave the presidency. The National Palace victory by the FSLN had damaged Somoza's image at home and abroad while greatly enhancing the image of the Sandinista Front. Once again, however, Somoza would not be moved. Given the existing weakness of Nicaragua's economy, the decline of foreign investment, flight of domestic capital, and diminishing domestic buying power due to expanding unemployment, the strike made no significant additional impact on the dictator.

For many businessmen and workers the month of August is an especially "dead period," since there is no cotton or coffee harvest at that time of the year. While some farmers and peasants are busy planting crops, it is a time of relative inactivity, so much so that the business sector takes its vacations in August. Thus,

> Never was there a bosses' strike that cost the owners of business establishments so little! It wasn't an heroic gesture on their part....They closed their doors primarily out of simple economic necessity rather than as a political protest."[1]

This idle period also meant that thousands of Nicaragua's labor force were unemployed, suffering with their families at home. This was particularly true of the poor workers in cities on the Pacific coast that are dependent on cotton and coffee production. The inactivity of this period allowed thousands of angry workers in these areas to collaborate in what was to become the September insurrection of 1978.

The insurrection actually began at the end of August in the city of Matagalpa. The coffee, cattle, and milk-producing center of 61,000 inhabitants has a history of rebelliousness that goes back to the indigenous uprising of

A Matagalpa street the day before the insurrection began.

provided the people with crucial barricades against the National Guard in urban centers across the country.

1881, the so-called "War of the Communeros" against their slave-like conditions under the lash of the large landowners.[2] Matagalpa, located in Nicaragua's central mountain range, had also been one of Sandino's bases in 1927. Now in 1978, it was Matagalpa's turn—just as it had been Monimbó's the previous February—to become "the front within the front" of the September insurrection.[3] On August 28 the young people of Matagalpa, their faces covered with bandanas, began to attack the National Guard. Armed with only pistols, rifles, and contact bombs, they forced the Guardsmen off the streets and back into the protection of their barracks, and immediately took over those sections of the city vacated by the retreating troops. In this way, they held out against the Guard through the first days of September, setting a model which other cities followed in the days to come.

The Matagalpa uprising accomplished two things: first, it alerted the FSLN to the fact that the Nicaraguan people, however ill-prepared, were ready to move openly against Somoza's forces. Second, it advised the young people in other cities that the time had come to carry out a coordinated nationwide attack against the dictatorship. The Insurrectionalists had called for this kind of general uprising over the objections of the other tendencies, and when the people of Matagalpa moved so decisively, the entire FSLN quickly responded to this popular initiative.[4]

On September 9, between 6:30 and 7:00 p.m., the insurrection erupted simultaneously in four other cities: Masaya, Managua, Chinandega and León. (Estelí joined the battle the following day.)[5] As soon as the sun had set but

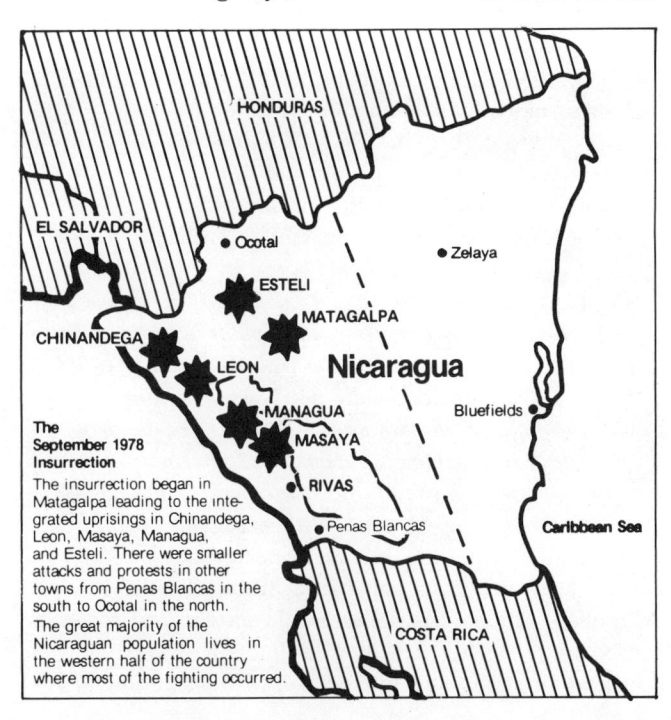

The September 1978 Insurrection

The insurrection began in Matagalpa leading to the integrated uprisings in Chinandega, Leon, Masaya, Managua, and Esteli. There were smaller attacks and protests in other towns from Penas Blancas in the south to Ocotal in the north.
The great majority of the Nicaraguan population lives in the western half of the country where most of the fighting occurred.

darkness forced the Guard to return to the safety of its barracks, the civilian forces, now backed by FSLN regulars, took over the urban centers (except in the case of Managua) and set up military positions at key locations. In each city *"los muchachos,"* along with Sandinista guerillas, blocked off highways, barricaded streets, and surrounded National Guard headquarters. When morning came, the Guard found itself unable to move. Because the military was divided and fighting so many battles at once, it was forced into a defensive struggle. Days passed before Somoza's forces could regain total control of Nicaragua's principal cities.

This insurrectional struggle was one of courage and creativity against overwhelming odds. In Masaya, the people again seized the central section of their city near San Jerónimo church, along with the whole *barrio* of Monimbó. In Managua, four sections of the city were taken over while a number of Guard barracks were burned to the ground. In the north, the FSLN first occupied the town of Chichigalpa and then moved on, joined by the urban militia and townspeople to occupy the city of Chinandega. In León, a coordinated attack by the people and the Sandinistas held Nicaragua's second-largest city for days.

The popular support was massive. Barricades were raised everywhere; public buildings were taken over; barracks, vehicles, stores and businesses were occupied. The Sandinista militia and popular organizations controlled urban centers as the Guard retreated to its quarters. Feeding and health needs were administered with the help of the whole population. The insurrectional offensive, whose weapons were enormously disproportionate to those of the Guard, was, nonetheless, able to break up army units at their regular posts."[6]

This initial advantage, although spectacular, did not last long as the people's struggle quickly turned into a defensive "war of positions."[7] As the National Guard rallied its forces and began to retake one city at a time, the FSLN, not yet prepared for an all-out confrontation with a standing army, had to retreat in order to save itself for the next encounter. This left the *"muchachos"* isolated in the urban centers facing the sophisticated fire power of the National Guard alone. Even then, the Guard could not retake the cities until Somoza's air force had first submitted them to massive and systematic bombing.

Somoza's aerial bombardment concentrated on the most densely populated civilian areas, turning them into burning "Guérnicas." With entire city blocks in flames or ruins, thousands of civilians were forced to gather in make-shift Red Cross refugee centers or flee to other cities, to the mountains, or across the border into Honduras or Costa Rica. In Estelí—where the bombing was the most intense— an estimated 80% of the population fled the city.[8] Those

"Masaya: Liberated Territory."

Civilians fleeing the bombardment of Esteli.

courtesy, LA PRENSA

courtesy, LA PRENSA

who remained were subjected to a form of brutal "pacification" called *Operation Cleanup:*[9] tanks and troops went from street to street and from house to house forcing entire families, especially young people, out into the open where many were lined up and shot. Somoza's genocidal response, however, should be seen not only as a sign of his cruelty, but as a military necessity, so tenacious was the resistance.

Although the National Guard was finally able to regain military control over the country, the September insurrection proved to be disastrous for Somoza and a decisive victory for the FSLN. The bombardment of Nicaragua's major cities massacred thousands of civilians and cost Somoza the last thread of support from the middle and upper classes. It also completely alienated the people from the National Guard. Furthermore, the bombing brought upon the dictator the repudiation of the international community.

The Sandinista Front lost few of its units. Indeed, thousands of the young people who had fought in the cities now retreated into the hills or the underground, swelling the ranks of the FSLN.

The insurrection also moved the Nicaraguan people from being anti-Somocista to becoming pro-Sandinista:

Ideologically-speaking, as the masses engaged in the September insurrection they were reminded of Sandino and his army of workers and peasants; they recalled the attempted pacts with Somoza and the January uprisings, the barricades and ongoing repression, the "civic" battles and the armed struggle of their vanguard. From their radical anti-somocismo, the masses emerged as a revolutionary people, joining the ranks of a nationalist and anti-imperialist consciousness, and became active Sandinistas.[10]

"They have stopped the insurrection, but the guerrilla action persists."

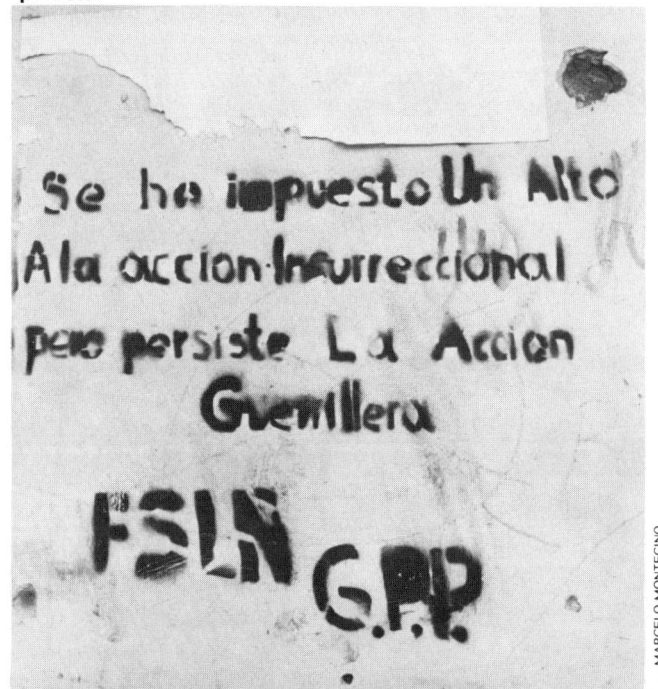

NICARAGUA'S GUERNICAS: NATIONAL GUARD BRUTALITY & THE REFUGEES

Somoza's National Guard obliterated countless human lives and extensive property in an effort to halt the nationwide September rebellion. The shocked international community used "genocide" to describe the horror of streets reduced to ashes and the stench of burning flesh which characterized four of Nicaragua's major cities. Costa Rican reports referred to the holocaust as Nicaragua's *guernicas.*[1] Guard repression was not a new experience for the Nicaraguan people, but the unprecedented extent of the destruction crushed any hopes that the Guard would turn against Somoza rather than accept the extreme orders to destroy their own cities and massacre the populace.[2]

In the summer months of 1978, institutionalized Guard repression increased in direct response to the rise in popular anger and protest. The Nicaraguan Commission on Human Rights (CPDH) described this as a move from "military abuse" to extreme human violations.[3] CPDH reported Guard atrocities such as rape and sexual abuse of young girls and pregnant women. In August alone, the Commission documented:

   89 assassinations by the National Guard
329 civilians jailed without charge
151 reported wounded in Guard confrontations
   24 adults disappeared
   34 children disappeared
   24 illegal break-ins, including churches, commercial centers, and entire neighborhoods.[4]

Peasants were routinely subjected to degrading searches and indiscriminate killings.

The genocide of September supported the Commission's August analysis of the Somoza government as unable to "maintain control using civilized methods, and incapable of establishing a way out of the crisis which has even a semblance of democracy."[5]

September's Statistics

Actual figures of September *guernicas* can only be estimated, as the government released no figures of civilian casualties, grossly understated National Guard casualties, and censored the efforts of others to document or aid the war victims. Even Red Cross workers became victims as they tried to minister to the wounded and remove dead bodies. In some instances they were denied entrance into war zones; outside of Leon two Red Cross volunteers were killed when National Guardsmen machine-gunned their clearly marked Red Cross vehicle.[6]

The Nicaraguan Commission on Human Rights report for September accused the Guard of:

arrest without accusation;
disappearance of prisoners;
appearances of cadavers of prisoners in deserted areas;
death from torture in jails;
civilians murdered without cause in the streets;
sexual abuse of women;
bombing whole neighborhoods to ruins.[7]

Acknowledging the impossibility of compiling accurate statistics, the Red Cross, Human Rights Commission, and other human rights groups published what little data they could gather. The Red Cross calculated September's death toll at 5,000, with more than 10,000 injured and 25,000 homeless. Behind the uncertain figures estimating the Guard's brutality lay the documented testimonies of thousands of suffering families and individuals. One exemplary story came from Leon on September 14:

About nine a.m. they approached the barrio San Juan from the north of the park...and began doing something no one ever expected. Armed men of the guard...entered the houses and pulled out males of all ages, even some who were only 12 to 15 years of age. The men were forced to kneel in rows with their hands on their heads. Some begged for their children, some for their mothers, others for their wives or brothers and sisters. But their cries were in vain. Men who had children in their arms were forced to place them apart.... Those who refused were killed with their children. Older children were lined up against the wall of their houses and machine-gunned. Mothers and grandmothers who came out to intercede for their children were also killed while embracing their adolescents. In almost every part of that sector of the city, the houses were destroyed....As if that were not enough, after everything was over, they forced the people to go out into the streets and clear up the debris. This included the dead bodies which the people were forced to place in piles on the sidewalks and to set on fire.[8]

42

Political prisoners in the Managua Police Headquarters.

The Human Rights Commission of the Organization of American States, sent to study the situation following the insurrection, dramatically concluded:

The Government of Nicaragua is responsible for serious attempts against the right to life, in violation of international humanitarian norms, by repressing in an excessive and disproportionate the manner the insurrections that occurred in September in the main cities of the country. In fact, the bombing of towns by the National Guard was done in an indiscriminate fashion and without prior evacuation of the civilian population, which caused innumerable deaths of persons who were not involved in the conflict.

Likewise, the Government is responsible for a large number of deaths which occurred after the combats, because of abuses perpetrated by the National Guard during the so-called "Operation Clean-Up" and other actions several days after the cessation of hostilities. Many persons were executed in a summary and collective fashion for the mere reason of living in neighborhoods where there had been activity by the FSLN; young people and defenseless children were killed.[9]

Refugees in Costa Rica and Honduras: "From Death Unto Death"

Somoza's destruction of commercial and residential areas in every major city, followed closely by the National Guard's "Operation Clean-Up," left thousands of Nicaraguans homeless and desperate. An estimated 60,000 persons sought asylum in other Central American countries—mainly in neighboring Costa Rica and Honduras.[10]

Hundreds of middle and upper class Nicaraguans were able to escape across the borders and rent hotel rooms or homes for the subsequent months, but the poor—who numbered in the tens of thousands and had suffered the most repression—had no place to go.

As Central American political cartoons so aptly expressed, the Nicaraguans had escaped near-death only to meet it again in the refugee camps.[11] Lacking the infrastructure to absorb a doubling or tripling of their population, cities along the borders sought Red Cross, United Nations, and other international assistance to cope with the problem. The conditions in the hundreds of hastily erected camps were little better than the situation left behind in smoldering Nicaragua. The daily trauma was both physical and psychological. Lack of food, water, sanitation facilities, and medical attention characterized most camps. Added to this was the lack of jobs, inactivity, a disproportionate number of children and older people, and constant fear of deportation or National Guard infiltration in search of *Sandinistas*.

The Honduran government, unsympathetic towards the FSLN, delayed the supply of even the minimal provisions to refugee camps on its soil. The United Nations High Commision on Refugees reported that some 15,000 Nicaraguans had received 3-month stay permits, but the number

Refugee camp in Costa Rica.

of non-registered refugees pushed that figure much higher. Of the 15,000, 10,000 needed urgent assistance.[12] A Mexican nurse described her first impressions of a border camp as "children with distended abdomens, malnourished and dehydrated, babies with extremely high fevers, desperate mothers, adults whose bodies constantly tremble in shock, crying in pain."[13] Rumors of spies and witnesses to deportations kept the psychological trauma at an intense level also. An international delegation visiting the Honduran camps in November reported:

We are convinced that the problems the Nicaraguan refugees face in Honduras are extremely serious. The alternatives they have at this moment are, to slowly die in their present inhuman conditions, or to return in desperation to Nicaragua with all the danger this implies.[14]

Nicaraguans in Costa Rica fared slightly better, primarily because the Costa Rican government and people supported the Sandinistas. The Government's special Coordinating Committee supervised "Operation Exodus," the refugee assistance project, and called for unrestricted border openings, medical assistance, and 60-day renewable permission papers. Upwards of 30,000 Nicaraguans arrived in the border camps before the year ended.

In spite of the efforts of the Costa Rican people to help the physical needs of the refugees, the fear of Somoza haunted them daily.

Monday evening when I visited the refugees I saw four young men in their early twenties. They were lying on mattresses in the middle of the church floor, one with his boots on, their hands behind their heads looking around at people, not saying a word. One of the sisters came over to me saying she thought they were spies. A mother told me the following day that she was concerned about the four men and wanted them checked out. One of the Costa Rican guards came into the church, looked over the situation, then said good night and left. But he returned through the back door and observed awhile. Then he went to the four, told them to get up and leave with him. He found three small bombs and several small hand guns. The feeling here is that Somoza is trying to terrorize the refugees and those of us working with them.

Tuesday evening two young women came into the church. They were checked out immediately and found to be "prostitutes" admitted to be receiving $50 a day to come across the border and get information from guards and other men in the camps.[15]

The refugee situation worsened before the struggle ended. Towns such as El Triunfo, with a population of 3,000 gave refuge to 11,000 Nicaraguans. The total number of refugees swelled to an incredible 100,000 before victory in July, 1979 ended their exile. Within a few weeks of that victory, 75% of those refugees would return to their homeland and begin a new life.

ORGANIZING THE URBAN MASSES: THE CDC

The FSLN and the Nicaraguan people learned several hard lessons from the September insurrection. They had lost many civilian lives in Somoza's vengeful scramble to regain control over the masses. From that time on, the people decisively rejected any further pretense of negotiating with Somoza and the National Guard (as the FAO continued to do), and allied themselves firmly with the FSLN. The Sandinistas realized, however, that if the civilian population was going to carry the struggle forward, defend itself against National Guard retaliation, and provide a support base for the FSLN forces, it had to be better organized. Many of the September casualties resulted from a lack of coordination within the neighborhoods which rose up against Somoza and from the inability of the relatively small FSLN forces to come into every street to defend the ill-prepared civilian population against the National Guard.

Following an analysis of the insurrection experience in late September, Civilian Defense Committees (CDC's) were created by the MPU and the FSLN to meet this need for coordinating and concretizing civilian resistance. The actual work of organizing the urban sector into these civilian committees fell to the MPU. The MPU already had paper unity in the form of its charter; now that charter would become grounded in grassroots support and cooperation.

The CDCs were defined with the following structure, goals and tasks. They would be organized by block, and coordinated by neighborhood and zonal steering committees. The directors and representatives to the steering committees would be democratically elected. The goals of the CDCs on the organizational plane were, 1) to effectively coordinate urban forces for defense against the National Guard; and 2) to place all resources and forces at the service of the popular brigades and armed forces combating the dictatorship, and on the political plane, 3) to establish a base which would eventually insure the people's power in a new social and political structure.[1]

During October, November, and December, with these goals before them, the people began intensive clandestine organizing. The increasingly paranoid National Guard stepped up its repressive military surveillance of the civilian population, forcing the MPU further underground.

While it seemed on the surface that the people's militant confrontation had somewhat abated, they were actually engaged in intensive activity laying the groundwork for even greater civilian resistance against the sophisticated military apparatus of the Guard in the near future.

A multitude of tasks faced the CDCs during the last months of 1978. The MPU visited neighborhoods having a history of militancy and shared the lessons learned by these residents with CDCs across the country so all could benefit from them. The CDCs collected medicines and first aid supplies, and trained older men and women in rudimentary first aid skills to tend the wounded. Basic foodstuffs were stored up, and reserve water supplies located. "Sandinista dining rooms" were organized where the combatants could come for nourishment during the fighting. "Security houses" were designated where key FSLN leadership could meet.

Every person accepted a task. Some watched and reported on National Guard movement. Others reported the activities of Somoza's spies. Older persons and young children acted as messengers between the Committees in different blocks and neighborhoods, maintaining constant communication between the CDCs and the FSLN. The Popular Brigades—combatants who had not formally joined the FSLN—took responsibility for being ready at a moment's notice to dig street trenches and take up the street bricks to build barricades.[2] Stores of home made weapons, such as molotov cocktails and "contact bombs" were made. Students built arsenals of arms and munitions seized in temporary take-overs of National Guard command posts.

Because the National Guard entered any private home at will, and often resorted to aerial bombardment or setting fire to whole neigborhoods in order to force people into the streets, the CDCs established evacuation passageways by connecting each house, through hidden wall openings and tunnels.

While the FAO and the upper class business opposition was scrambling to consolidate its bourgeois forces, taking advantage of Somoza's weakened political position following the September insurrection, the MPU and CDCs developed into a unified, clandestine urban civilian and political force. They were well on the way to being prepared to battle the National Guard on the streets; they were also prepared to battle the United States' mediation efforts and the FAO's call for a plebiscite. The consolidation of Civilian Defense Committees gave the masses their first real experience with democratic process and cooperative organization. Politically they were clear that neither the U.S. nor the FAO would be allowed to manipulate the struggle to effect a change of Somoza the man, without an eradication of the structure of *somocismo*.

THE U.S. MEDIATION EFFORT & THE ROLE OF THE FAO

Soon after the Nicaraguan people began to dig themselves out of the disaster of Somoza's genocidal response to the September insurrection, the United States initiated efforts to find an alternative to the dictatorship. By early October, the Carter Administration received approval from the Organization of American States (OAS) to set up a "Trinational Commission for Friendly Cooperation"[1] involving the United States, the Dominican Republic and Guatemala—two countries the Administration knew could be convinced to support its imperialist strategy. This "mediation team"—implying mediation between Somoza and his "legitimate opposition" in the Broad Opposition Front (FAO)—sought an alternative to the Somoza family which would leave intact the interests and structures created by Somoza, including the National Guard. This alternative is technically referred to as *somocismo*.

It was therefore natural that the first Nicaraguan organization to respond to this U.S. initiative should be the anti-Somoza business community which had created the FAO. Joined by some liberal organizations on October 5, the FAO made a formal declaration encouraging support for such mediation which it directed to "the heroic and patriotic Nicaraguan people, who at the cost of the sacrifice and blood-shedding of its best sons and daughters, struggled to overthrow the Somoza dictatorship in order to establish a regime of justice and democracy in our country."[2]

This call for mediation by the FAO was based on a series of presumptions which revealed the political parameters of the organization:

1. The National Strike (the business work stoppage which began in August) lasting 31 days had been "a great success;"
2. The attacks by Somoza's National Guard against six cities constituted an "indiscriminate aggression" against the Nicaraguan people;
3. Notwithstanding U.S. military and political aggression in the past and without questioning U.S. motives at this time the Nicaraguan people should support conversations towards mediation through this international body (the Trinational Commission);
4. Such support does not imply dialogue nor a pact with Somoza the man nor with *somocismo*, but rather that his family must go and his dictatorship must be dismantled;
5. These conversations, which will be carried out by the United States or the OAS, aimed at finding "mediation formulas" that will lead to the profound process of democratic reforms which our people seek, should involve no tricks; and
6. These conversations should be carried out within the climate of individual guarantees and freedom of the press and radio so that everyone will know what is going on.[3]

These statements make clear that the leadership of the FAO sought little more than a reform of the Somoza system. However, since that system had been entrenched for so long and was still so powerful, to some middle and upper class Nicaraguans these proposals sounded like a significant change.

This mediation effort indicated that the United States government recognized the September insurrection as a watershed for Somoza. His repressive response had seriously eroded his international image and, more importantly, the September bombings had probably made it impossible for Somoza to maintain national control. The U.S. government also knew that the long-standing links between

U.S. capital and Nicaragua's upper class were breaking down as a result of the intensifying class struggle; a popular revolution was in the making.[4] Since the U.S.' agent in Nicaragua (Somoza) could no longer guarantee a climate of stability for foreign investment, some political alternative was necessary. However, precisely because the Somozas had been such faithful protectors of U.S. interests for 44 years, the Carter Administration had to approach this transfer of powers cautiously. At the same time, Somoza's ego and adamant refusal to resign required specific pressures.

The Carter strategy included, therefore, "the application of pressures and incentives to force our erstwhile client dictator to go into early retirement."[5] These pressures consisted of:

1. stopping all 'pipeline' military aid;[6]
2. blocking loans from the International Monetary Fund (Somoza had requested $20 million from the IMF in the Fall of 1978) to his nearly bankrupt regime;[7] and,
3. threatening to cut off diplomatic relations.[8]

For incentive, if Somoza responded favorably, he would be granted asylum in the United States with the right to bring with him some of the vast fortune he had amassed off the exploitation of the Nicaraguan people and nation.[9] Over the next few months, this mediation strategy would be constantly frustrated by Somoza's indecision about whether or not he would respond to U.S. pressure.

Internally, the key to the success of the mediation process rested squarely on the FAO—the alternative power structure being groomed to replace the dictatorship. This does not mean the United States agreed with all sixteen points of the FAO's program, which included among others: a new national army serving the people; eradication of *somocista* corruption; the end of all repressive laws; freedom for political prisoners and the return of foreign exiles; a true agrarian reform; a reform of the fiscal system; the restructuring of the judicial system.[10] Even though these improvements seem quite progressive, they were general enough not to cause undue alarm to the U.S. upper classes or to the State Department. They contained, for instance, no criticism of U.S. imperialism and no suggestion of any change in class relations. On the contrary, nine of the sixteen points called for the restructuring of the judicial-political system along lines that would merely reform the military dictatorship. In fact, even the FAO leadership qualified its own projections by reflecting semi-hopefully:

We want an efficient and reasonable State, without acts of contraband or fraud, with a political economy that benefits everyone, and one that is preferably democratic. But if that is not possible, we want at least a military dictatorship that is able to maintain fully the image of democracy and one that can guarantee order so that all may live in peace. Amen.[11]

While the FAO genuinely sought an end to the Somoza regime, it was more concerned about containing the rapidly developing process of radicalization at the popular level within limits acceptable to the business community. The reverberations of the September insurrection went far deeper than merely creating a chaotic social environment; they had created profound psychological and political changes within the society. At the psychological level, the Nicaraguan people had moved from anti-Somoza hatred; they were now determined to create a Sandinista future. On the other hand, the upper classes had moved from deep concern to desperation. In political terms, the insurrection had resulted in *the disintegration of bourgeois unity coupled with the consolidation of proletarian forces.*

This serious challenge required an extended interim period during which Somoza could re-establish military consolidation over the rebellious society, using ferocious repression. The long and delayed mediation process (from September 15 to November 30) provided the proper "democratic" cover for this re-stabilization process. The anti-Somoza position of the Carter Administration did not imply, however, any weakening of support for the National Guard. The United States stopped sending arms directly but refused to put pressure on Israel and Argentina to stop their arms flow to Nicaragua.

At the same time, vacillating U.S. State Department officials underestimated the breadth of FSLN support and the resoluteness of the popular forces. Thus, instead of wooing the progressive liberal faction within the FAO, it only exacerbated the situation by supporting the conservative sector, that is, the INDE and COSEP business sector. The political nature of this conservatism was reflected in a statement by the former President of Costa Rica, Jose Figueres (who was assisting the U.S. mediation effort)—a statement which was released as early as September 22 by a senior officer of the State Department:

> *Of course, we must avoid another Cuba, and we don't want another mess like the invasion of the Dominican Republic. We've been looking everywhere for another Balaguer* (the U.S.-supported strongman who ran a "controlled democracy" in the Dominican Republic from 1966-1978) *but we can't seem to locate him.*"[12]

The right-wing tendencies of the U.S.-dominated mediation team were evident from the very start of the mediation process and caused distrust among liberal factions of the FAO. That is why "The Twelve"—the only group in the FAO with direct links with the Sandinistas—withdrew from the mediation efforts by the end of October, charging that the team was working "to impose a docile government to the United States' liking."[13] Following their lead, during November one by one the other liberal organizations also withdrew: the Independent Liberal Party (PLI), the social democratic trade union federation (CTN), the Christian Democrats (PPSC), and the Nicaraguan Socialist Party (PSN). This left the FAO without any popular base of support.

The United States tried to counter this abandonment of the FAO by reporting that the mediation conversations were going well. In fact, by the end of November only the conservative FAO and the Liberal Party were still in dialogue. At this point, Somoza suggested holding a plebiscite and the United States quickly jumped at the new opening, as did the anti-Somoza upper class. If the Nicaraguan people could be brought to the polls, and assuming such a referendum would come out in Somoza's favor, a plebiscite could counter the negative impact of the September insurrection, weaken the leadership of the FSLN, and divide the growing popular solidarity in the urban and rural areas. The weakness in this referendum strategy was that in a country governed for decades by the Somozas, where elections had been so manipulated over the years, few Nicaraguans had any faith in the ballot. This made the United States' great December push for a plebiscite appear to be more a strategy geared to assuage North American public opinion rather than to force Somoza out of office.

Somoza was, of course, using the idea of a plebiscite for his own purposes, playing with the liberal pressures exerted

48

by both the FAO and the United States. Even the conservative FAO forces were skeptical, however, and would only accept a referendum on the basis of certain pre-conditions:
1. The Somoza family leave the country within 40 days;
2. A new head of the National Guard be named;
3. The OAS control the elections; and,
4. The FAO, the PLN (Somoza's party) and the OAS oversee the plebiscite.[14]

Despite these pressures, Somoza held fast to his "constitutional commitment" to remain in power until 1981. Even when he indicated some openness to sharing power or talked about leaving office, his statements included so many conditions, they were impossible to interpret. For example, on November 30, in response to the above FAO demands, he said:

> *"The demands of the opposition in Nicaragua were that I should abandon power and against that I proposed that there should be a plebiscite in which the parties would measure their respective forces and that we would divide executive power proportionately. This, of course, they have refused and thus the cooperative (mediation) Commission came forth with the proposal to hold a popular consultation about whether I should remain in power or not—something which my party is studying in order to decide how to respond. Once a plebiscite is held, such a process must involve prior proof of a situation indicative of my willingness to renounce my post. That is, if I am, in fact, defeated in such a plebiscite."*[15]

Such cynicism and double-talk represented a studied counter-strategy on Somoza's part, one which further discredited the mediation Commission and revealed the weakness of the Carter Administration's policy when its liberal pressures had no effect on this seasoned warrior.

The position of the left towards a plebiscite might have been to unite the people around a campaign to abstain from any electoral farce.[16] But the rejection of such a popular process could result in pacifying the masses rather than moving them to take the offensive, which they had already begun. This analysis led the FSLN and the MPU to decide on a strategy of *parallel power*,[17] that is, of providing a real alternative to the FAO. This was accomplished by creating the National Patriotic Front which united the FSLN, the MPU, and the progressive sectors of the FAO (which had left that coalition in November). It was the task of the MPU to mobilize its constituencies around this banner, which it did during December and January.

This popular mobilization against any pacts or plebiscites led Somoza to outrightly reject all U.S. urgings that he leave Nicaragua and, indeed, Somoza began attacking the United States for its unfaithfulness to an old ally. While the mediation Commission continued into the next year, by the end of 1978 it had become an empty structure that survived only through U.S. fiat. In fact, any mediation that involved Somoza had long since lost any political significance. It had absolutely no popular support within Nicaragua.

FOOTNOTES

The Assassination of Pedro Joaquín Chamorro

1. *La Prensa,* Managua, Nicaragua, January 11, 1978.
2. *La Prensa,* January 14, 1978.
3. *La Prensa,* January 15, 1978.
4. *La Prensa,* January 11, 1978.
5. *La Prensa,* January 9, 1978.
6. *La Prensa,* January 19, 1978
7. *La Prensa,* January 18, 1978.
8. *La Prensa,* January 23, 1978.
9. Mario García del Cueto, "Crimen y Pillage en el Imperio Económico-Político de Somoza," *Tricontinental Especial,* Havana, 1979, pp.42-43.
10. *The Guardian,* January 25, 1978.
11. Pedro Joaquín Chamorro, *Estirpe Sangrienta: Los Somozas,* 4th ed., Managua: Artes Graficas, 1958, p. XVI.

Business Work Stoppage and Popular Protest

1. *Encuentro: La Realidad Nacional,* Universidad Centroamericana, Managua, July-December, 1978. p. 18.
2. *La Prensa,* January 27, 1978.
3. *Novedades,* January 28, 1978.
4. *La Prensa,* January 30-31, 1978.
5. *Encuentro,* p. 23.
6. *Encuentro,* p. 23.
7. *Encuentro,* p. 23.
8. *La Prensa* and *Novedades,* February 4, 1978.
9. *La Prensa,* February 9, 1978.
10. *La Prensa,* February 11, 1978.
11. *Novedades,* February 9, 1978.

Monimbo: Flame of Popular Resistance

1. Comité Cristiano de Solidaridad con el Pueblo de Nicaragua (CRISOL), *Monimbó: Tragedia y Símbolo de Liberación,* Managua, February 1979, p. 5.
2. *Monimbó: Tragedia y Símbolo de Liberación,* introduction, p.2.
3. *La Prensa,* February 8, 1978.
4. *La Prensa,* February 11, 1978.
5. *La Prensa,* February 21, 1978.
6. *La Prensa,* February 22, 1978.
7. *La Prensa,* February 27, 1978.
8. *Unidad Sandinista,* Panamá, Año 1, No. 2, 1978.
9. *La Prensa,* February 27, 1978.
10. *La Prensa,* March 2, 1978.
11. *Monimbó: Tragedia y Símbolo de Liberación,* p.2.

Organizing the Campesinos: The ATC

1. "Nicaragua," *NACLA's North American and Empire Report,* Vol. X, No. 2 (February 1976), p.10.
2. *La ATC, Organización Sandinista de los Trabajadores del Campo, primera parte,* Colección Oscar Robelo, Folleto No. , Managua /éé, p.ª.
3. *El Machete,* Nicaragua, April 1978, No.1, p.3. (illegal, mimeographed FSLN publication).
4. *La ATC,* p.3.
5. *La ATC,* p.4.
6. *La ATC,* p.5.
7. *La ATC,* p. 5.
8. *La ATC,* p. 2.
9. *La ATC, Organización de Trabajadores del Campo,* Segunda parte, Colección Oscar Robelo, Folleto No. 6, Managua, 1979. p. 3.
10. *La ATC,* Segunda parte, p.3.

NOTE: Little written material was available at the time of this writing which could document the development of Nicaragua's campesino movement. The information compiled here came from the first post-victory documents of the Asociación de Trabajadores del Campo (ATC) in Managua, and EPICA interviews with ATC workers, and with U.S. and British missionaries who worked in rural Nicaragua between 1968 and 1979.

Student Mobilization Against the Dictatorship

1. Nicaraguan Revolutionary Youth (JRN), "Participación de la Juventud en la Lucha Popular Contra la Dictadura Somocista," November 1978, p. 5., n.p., (mimeographed document)
2. Short strategy sessions on campus which were terminated before authorities could break them up.
3. EPICA interview, Washington, D.C., December 1979.
4. This was a kind of mustard gas used during WWI which did not cause death but was an extreme irritant causing vomiting, burning eyes and prolonged incapacity to fight.
5. *Recuperación,* or recovery, is a technical phrase coined by the FSLN to refer to all arms, equipment, money and food supplies taken over expressly for the revolution. It was a concept expressing the right of the people and the vanguard to take for the struggle what Somoza had stolen from them.
6. *Lucha Sandinista,* Publication of the Foreign Affairs Commission of the FSLN, June 3, 1978.

The Role of Women in the Revolution: AMPRONAC

1. *Documentos de AMPRONAC,* Managua, November 1978, p.2. (mimeographed, unpublished pamphlet).
2. *La Prensa,* October 3, 1977.
3. *Nicaraguan Constitution,* Articles 40, 41, 42, and 71.
4. *La Prensa,* October 22, 1977.
5. *La Prensa,* December 6, 1977.
6. *La Prensa,* December 27, 1977.
7. *La Prensa,* January 26, 1977.
8. *Documentos de AMPRONAC,* p. 5.
9. *La Prensa,* March 8, 1978.
10. *Documentos de AMPRONAC,* p.5.
11. *La Prensa,* March 8, 1978.
12. *La Prensa,* March 10, 1978.
13. *Documentos de AMPRONAC,* p.7.
14. *La Prensa,* April 10, 1978.
15. *La Prensa,* April 10, 11, 12, 1978.

The Consolidation of Popular Forces: The MPU

1. "Programa Inmediato del MPU," *Nicaragua: Reforma ó Revolución,* Managua, n.p., n.d., p.131.
2. "Manifesto del Nacimiento del Movimiento Pueblo Unido." *July 1978 (mimeographed, illegal publication somewhere in Nicaragua).*
3. "Manifesto."
4. EPICA interview with Commander Carlos Somora, Chinandega, October 1979.
5. EPICA interview with Somora.
6. Felipe Mantica Abaunza, Nicaraguan Chamber of Commerce; Joaquín Cuadra Chamorro, Corporation lawyer; Miguel D'Escoto, Maryknoll priest; Ricardo Coronel Kautz, agronomist; Carlos Tunnerman, Rector of the National university; Fernando Cardenal, Jesuit priest; Emilio Baltodano Pallais, Pres., Nicaraguan Commission on Human Rights; Sergio Ramirez, lawyer; Arturo Cruz, banker; Carlos Gutierrez Sotelo, dental surgeon; Ernesto Castillo lawyer; and Casimiro Sotelo, architect and urban developer.
7. Mayo Antonio Sanchez, *Nicaragua, Año Cero,* Mexico: Editorial Diana, July 1979, pp. 137-138.
8. *Nicaragua: Reforma ó Revolución,* p.106.
9. "Manifesto."
10. *La Prensa,* July 28, 1978.
1. "Manifesto."
12. "Puntos Programáticos del Pueblo Unido," (attached to the Manifesto.)
13. *La Prensa,* July 28, 1978.

Attack on the National Palace

1. Gabriel García Marquez, "Casa de los Chanchos," *Sandino Vive; Nicaragua Vencerá,* Panamanian Committee of Solidarity with Nicaragua, Panamá, September 1978, pp. 3-7, 24.

The September Insurrection of 1978

1. *Nicaragua: Reforma ó Revolución,* Part III, p.111
2. *Sandino Vive; Nicaragua Vencerá,* no.3, September 1978, p.9.
3. *Sandino Vive; Nicaragua Vencerá,* p.8.
4. *Nicaragua: Reforma ó Revolución,* part III, p.111.
5. *Nicaragua: Reforma ó Revolución,* p.114.
6. *Nicaragua: Reforma ó Revolución,* p.115.
6. *Pensamiento Crítico; La Lucha de Clases en Nicaragua,* vol. 1, Managua, n.p., 1979. pp.53-54.

Nicaragua's Guernicas: National Guard Brutality and the Refugees

1. Victor Sanabria Documentation Center, San José, Costa Rica, comparing the destruction of the Spanish town of Guernica in the Spanish Civil War to the 6 cities in Nicaragua.
2. *Washington Post,* September 25, 1978.
3. Permanent Commission on Human Rights, *"Formas y Alcances de la Violación a los Derechos Humanos en Nicaragua,"* Managua, March 3, 1979, p.2.
4. Victor Sanabria Documentation Center, *"Presentación del Segundo Informe Sobre Derechos Humanos en Nicaragua,"* San José, Costa Rica (August 1978) p.1
5. "Formas y Alcances," p.7.
6. *Washington Post,* September 16, 1978.
7. "Formas y Alcances," p.1.
8. Victor Sanabria Documentation Center, "Tercer Informe." Testimony included as mimeographed addendum.
9. Inter-American Commission on Human Rights of the OAS, "Report on the Situation of Human Rights in Nicaragua: Findings of the On-site Observation Team," Washington, D.C. October, 1978.
10. Permanent Secretariat on Human Rights in Central America, "Special Bulletin About the Judgement of Somoza as a War Criminal," San José, Costa Rica, November 15, 1978.
11. Informativo CENCOS-CIILA, "Honduras: Continua la Represión en los Campos de Refugiados Nicaraguenses," Mexico, May 11, 1979, p.12.
12. United Nations High Commission on Refugees, "Report on the Refugee Situation in Latin America," 1978-79. New York, New York.
13. *"Honduras: Continua la Represión,"* p.5.
14. "Special Bulletin on the Judgment of Somoza, Nicaraguan Refugees in Costa Rica and Honduras," p.3.
15. *Unpublished letters written by a Catholic priest working in the northern Costa Rican camps, October 1978.*

Organizing the Urban Masses: the CDC

1. *"Atención!!! Pueblo de Nicaragua,"* FSLN Proletariano, September 1978, (mimeographed, illegal publication).
2. These *adoquines* were commonly referred to as "Somoza Bricks" because his private factory monopolized their manufacture. All major roads in Nicaragua were paved with them.

The U.S. Mediation Effort and the Role of the FAO

1. *Latin American Political Report,* London, October 6, 1978, p.311.
2. "Declaration of the Broad Opposition Front, FAO" Nanagua, October 5, 1978, p.1. (mimeographed flyer).
3. "Declaration of the FAO," p.1-2.

4. *Nicaragua: Reforma ó Revolución,* Part III, p.141.
5. Thomas Walker, "An Evaluation of the Carter Administration's Human Rights Policy in Nicaragua," Ohio University, fall 1979, p.22. (unpublished report).
6. *Latin America Political Report,* no.27, September 22, 1978, p.289.
7. Alejandro Bendana, "Crisis in Nicaragua," *NACLA,* Nov.-Dec. 1978, p.32.
8. "Nicaragua: Troubled Economy," *Central America Report,* no. 42, San Francisco, October 23, 1978, p.329.
9. Walker, p.25.
10. "Programa Democrático del Gobierno Nacional del FAO," Managua, October 1978, (mimeographed).
11. *Pensamiento Crítico: Lucha de Clases en Nicaragua,* p.48
12. Walker, p.25.
13. *Latin American Political Report,* no.43, November 3, 1978, p.342.
14. Leo Gabriel and Oscar Davila, "El FAO Acepta el Plebiscito," Managua, November 30, 1978. (mimeographed flyer).
15. *Nicaragua: Reforma ó Revolución,* p.151.
16. *Nicaragua: Reforma ó Revolución,* p.153.

MADRE

SI MAÑANA, MADRE MIA
LA MUERTE ME DOBLARA EN LA TRINCHERA
NO LLORES.
LA NIÑA DE TU VIENTRE
SERIA MI CADAVER
MI SANGRE SE CONVERTIRA EN SONIDO
Y MI VIDA SERA UN GRITO
HECHO BANDERA.

II

SI MAÑANA LOS ESBIRROS
ENTREGARAN EN TUS MANOS
MI CUERPO MASACRADO
NO LLORES
SIENTE QUE TE DA ORGULLO
QUE TU DISTES A LA PATRIA
UN HIJO QUE NO QUISO SER ESCLAVO
QUE PREFIRIO EL SILENCIO
DE LOS SIGLOS
ANTES DE GEMIR
BAJO EL LATIGO DEL VERDUGO

PART 2

January 1979 - Victory

THE NATIONAL PATRIOTIC FRONT: THE PEOPLE'S PARALLEL POWER STRUCTURE

January 1979 was a political turning point in the popular resistance. The MPU's earlier hard work, particularly through the Civilian Defense Committees, had the masses fully organized and working democratically. The CDCs were now a base for political opposition to the discredited and depleted FAO. The FSLN recognized that the time was ripe to consolidate its challenge to the dictatorship and establish an alternative political structure: the National Patriotic Front (FPN).

1979 begins, then, with gratifying if not triumphant prospects. We know we have before us a hard battle. But we also know that the popular positions are solidifying and taking on an expression of concrete political and military organization, while the contradictions in the dictatorship's crisis are sharpening and the pact-making conciliatory politicians find their manuevers reduced with every move they make.[1]

While the FSLN mounted its political offensive, Somoza tightened the reign of military control. His strict "black code" censorship of radio and press made dissemination of information erratic and incomplete.

Entire families were murdered in rural areas surrounding Estelí, and the National Guard indiscriminately fired on civilian groups in the streets.[2] International press cables reported that 200 persons died during the first 24 days of 1979.[3]

Despite the repression, the resistance took advantage of Somoza's weakened political position and won several major political gains. First of all, the MPU and other civic organizations announced their intent to commemorate the anniversary of Chamorro's death. On January 6, Somoza forbade any public assembly in Chamorro's memory, but withdrew the command three days later when the people threatened to disregard the dictator's orders, regardless of the consequences. The MPU viewed Somoza's vacillation as a major victory for the people, and on January 10, the country observed a general work stoppage and 30,000 people marched in Managua.

Somoza suffered a second political defeat by the Health Workers Federation (Fetsalud). Thirty Fetsalud workers staged a three-week hunger strike in January to protest the firing of 2800 hospital workers charged with participating in the national strike the previous August. The resulting publicity and pressure from other opposition sectors forced the regime to order all the Fetsalud workers rehired.[4]

Finally, when the dictatorship announced that university funds would be eliminated from the 1979 national budget, teachers and students responded immediately, demanding 6% of the budget for the universities. Up until this time these groups had worked independently of one another. The organizational ties created between these student and teacher organizations consolidated a major sector of the civilian resistance, increasing their effectiveness in other areas of the struggle.[5]

Somoza lost ground on the military and international fronts as well. At home, the FSLN continued harassing the National Guard and successfully carried out a wave of bank robberies. The National Bank Association reported it had lost 14 million *cordobas* in January alone.[6] At the international level members of the Group of Twelve, which had renounced the FAO's mediation tactics, visited heads of state in Colombia, Venezuela, and Panama, with the result that the FSLN's credibility was strengthened.

MOTHER

If tomorrow, my mother,
Death should find me doubled over in a trench,
Don't weep.
The honor of your womb
Would then by my dead body.
My blood, the seed of new beginnings.
My life would then be a shout,
A flag symbolizing the struggle.

If tomorrow the enemy
Should place in your hands
My massacred body,
Don't weep.

Rather, be proud
That you gave our country
A son who would not be a slave,
Who preferred the silence
Of the centuries
To a moan produced
By the oppressor's lash.

Poem stencilled on a wall in Leon.

The Masses Open the Doors of Democracy

These political gains established the MPU firmly in a leadership role. Everyone agreed that it should serve as the base for creating the National Patriotic Front which would unite all the popular democratic forces, including the liberal groups which had withdrawn from the FAO and the mediation attempts the previous November.[7]

On January 11, the MPU's member organizations met with the Independent Liberal Party (PLI), the Group of Twelve, the Nicaraguan Workers Confederation (CTN), and the Managua Radio Reporters Union (SRPM). The Popular Social Christian Party and the Nicaraguan Democratic Movement (MDN) attended as official observers. At that meeting they outlined their minimal program which would unite "all democratic and progressive representative forces of the country."

1. Defense of national sovereignty and rejection of any foreign intervention;
2. Commitment to bring down the dictatorship;
3. Struggle for an effective democracy, justice and social progress.[8]

They formed a six-member National Secretariat consisting of three members of the MPU, one from the Group of Twelve, one from the Independent Liberal Party, and one from the Social Christian Party.

The formation of the Patriotic Front accomplished an important FSLN goal: a unification of all the anti-Somoza forces under the hegemony of the MPU.[9] The MPU considered the ideological integration of this popular democratic block no small feat:

With the unity of political forces from all our different organizations around the central objectives of anti-Somoza and the people's right to self-determination, we have overcome the obstacles which might otherwise have divided us. Placing great confidence in unified action, we are convinced that this phase of the struggle holds strategic importance.[10]

The National Patriotic Front's key function was to complement the ongoing military struggle with a public ideological battle.[11] The FPN openly challenged the bourgeois opposition, in particular its attack on the FAO's concessions to the United States government and its acceptance that the National Guard and Somoza's political party could participate in a new government.[12]

As soon as the FPN was formed, its commissions began organizing. One particularly successful commission, the Urban Workers Commission, formed a Workers Defense Committee (CDT). The CDT united workers unions such as the National Association of Teachers (ANDEN), the People's Union Movement (MSPT), and the National Employees Union (UNE). When Somoza devalued the *cordoba* by 43% in May, the CDT organized a major protest. It also addressed such issues as poor working conditions and low wages. Other FPN commissions mobilized around unemployment, lack of urban housing, and public transportation. Their purpose was to pressure the system when it was least able or willing to make social concessions.[13]

The FSLN and MPU did not consider the National Patriotic Front to be the final basis of a new government. At the appropriate time a provisional government would be formed based on the political principles outlined by the FSLN. Until then, throughout the spring and early summer 1979, the National Patriotic Front represented the Sandinistas' political alternative to the dictatorship.

RELIGIOUS MEDIATION & SOLIDARITY THE ROLE OF THE CHURCH

The Church's relation to the Nicaraguan revolution can only be examined fairly within an historical context. Two levels of internal processes determined the Church's response to the struggle against the dictatorship. Somoza's increasingly brutal and inhuman role moved both sectors— (1) the institutional hierarchy and (2) the parish priests and nuns, ministers and laity working at the base—to criticize the dictatorship. The Catholic hierarchy assumed a role of "mediator" and avoided taking a clear position, while the Protestants and Catholics working with the poor expressly opposed the dictatorship. One Catholic reflection of the Church's oscillation between mediation and solidarity noted:

For many reasons, the Catholic Church in Nicaragua has the power to make of this present situation an example for other Latin American churches, and for all Christian communities. (One) reason is that...the Church, in all its dimensions (hierarchy, pastoral agents, lay people) is seen by the masses as having opted for the interests of the poor....On the other side of the ledger is the hierarchy, not a total debit, but divided among itself and somewhat cut off from the lay religious and clergy at the base. [1]

This ambivalence is rooted in developments in Latin America during the 1960's when many priests, nuns, and laity moved into greater commitment and solidarity with the poor. The 1968 Medellín Conference of Latin American bishops reflected this commitment, encouraging the Church hierarchy to support and carry forward the existing grass roots work. One way in which the Church in Nicaragua responded the the Medellín mandates was to create a lay ministry called "Delegates of the Word," who acted out their Christian concern for the needs and problems of the poor. In doing so, the Church abandoned its traditional *status quo* position and became less supportive of Somoza. The more traditional and conservative native Nicaraguan parish priests would have little to do with the Delegates in the early years of the movement, while the more liberal foreign clergy welcomed their help. This tension between foreign and national clergy was part of the dynamic leading

Ernesto Cardenal, Poet priest who joined the FSLN.

to greater openness and change in the Church's involvement in the struggle.

The liberal social activists among Protestant (Evangelical) missionaries[2] in Nicaragua during the 1960's (mostly from the United States) were greatly influenced by the civil rights movement and the example of Martin Luther King. The German martyr Dietrich Bonhoeffer became their principal ethical guide and example. Applying Bonhoeffer's thinking to the Nicaraguan reality, some of these Evangelicals even likened Anastasio Somoza to Adolph Hitler.[3]

This liberal trend continued despite the setbacks during the mid-60's when a number of strongly anti-communist exiled Cuban pastors and teachers arrived. These Cubans campaigned against certain liberal pastors and successfully had some expelled from the country.[4]

The Earthquake and its Aftermath

The physical disaster and dislocation of thousands of Nicaraguans as a result of the 1972 earthquake led many Christian congregations and organizations to dedicate much of their time and resources to disaster relief. This humanitarian effort put the Church into much closer contact with the peoples' misery and the systemic violence of the Somoza regime. At the institutional level, Catholic Relief Services (CRS) and the Evangelical Committee for Aid and Development (CEPAD), channeled enormous amounts of U.S. church relief supplies and monies to earthquake victims and the poor. However, because Somoza siphoned off most of the international aid which would have begun the reconstruction process, the foreign charity of the churches and private groups could not significantly alleviate the suffering; in fact, social inequities actually increased. On the positive side, as Christians came in closer contact with the poor they grew in social consciousness and began to connect the immediate suffering of the masses with the systemic causes, i.e. Somoza and the Nicaraguan class structure.

The widespread repression during the state of siege following the earthquake was the breaking point for many Christians. Catholic young people protested openly against the Somoza regime and in many cases the church hierarchy defended the youth. There was no middle ground for reform under Somoza because every effort at change was labelled "Communism" or "communist inspired."[5] This spurred many traditional congregations into an ever-deepening commitment to the poor in their urban neighborhoods and *barrios*, while the "Delegates" were intensifying their efforts at social improvements among plantation workers and *campesinos*.

Assassination of Chamorro and the September Insurrection

Increasing numbers of Christians became involved in the struggle during the fall of 1977. As the repression increased, liberal sectors called for a National Dialogue. Mons. Obando y Bravo, who became a symbol of the sincere but ambivalent religious mediator, headed the Dialogue. As the Dialogue disintegrated before it could actually begin, however, many Christians moved from mediation to political protest against the violations of human rights. The upper class Christian women in AMPRONAC protested against the 350 *campesino* disappearances in the Atlantic region documented by the Capuchin Fathers. These popular and publicly supported models of Christian action were typified by a religious procession held on New Year's Day 1978, dedicated to peace in honor of "Christ the King." The procession of lay and religious people turned into a political march with banners reading: "Where are our *campesino* brothers and sisters?" and "Free all political prisoners!"

In the face of Somoza's mounting repression, the legitimacy of the church's mediation role rapidly disappeared. When Chamorro was assassinated on January 10, the most common slogan used by Christians was "there is no place for dialogue." The National Guard attacks on Christians attending the memorial services for Chamorro, particularly

Wreath marking the place of Chamorro's assassination.

against Monimbó women and children following a mass at San Sebastian church (February 1978), led the local parish priests into open support of the *muchachos* against the Guard. Progressive Catholics increasingly joined the more political "Christian Committee in Solidarity for Peace." Simultaneously, Mons. Obando y Bravo issued his three conditions under which it was legitimate to take up arms.[6]

The September 1978 insurrection served as a further radical break from traditional non-violent protests as hundreds of the young faithful joined the FSLN in the mountains or urban underground. By that time there were well-known Catholic leaders of this militant move: Ernesto Cardenal, whose humble community at Solentiname[7] had been destroyed by the National Guard the previous fall, had joined the FSLN; Miguel D'Escoto, an upper-class Maryknoll priest became an outspoken opponent of Somoza from within the political group "The Twelve;" and Gaspar Garcia Laviana, a Spanish priest from Tola and San Juan del Sur in the Department of Rivas, joined the FSLN following the example of the Colombian priest, Camilo Torres.

The "Quiet" Interlude Between September 1978 and April 1979

After the genocidal bombing in September, incredible popular energy went into hurried preparations for the next encounter between the people and the National Guard. The main instruments of local organizing during those months were the Civilian Defense Committees (CDCs). Many Christian congregations collaborated with the CDCs, either as members or sympathizers. Church buildings were offered as relief and medical centers, while Christians helped prepare food caches, built escape passageways, "recapture" supplies, and increase international solidarity contacts.

By February, Nicaragua's 2.3 million inhabitants had only 1,000 clergy and 300 lay persons serving them. However, the 300 laity had organized community groups involving some 5,000 Christian activists who now clearly worked for and with the people. As the National Conference of Religious (CONFER) said, "In Nicaragua, any examination of public opinion will show that there is a favorable confidence among the people toward the Church, because the Church has refused to be an accomplice of the oppressors."[8]

In mid-February 1979, the National Guard brutally assassinated five unarmed young people hiding inside León's El Calvario parish church. Mons. Marcelino Areas and all the clergy of León sent a telegram to Somoza repudiating the act and demanding an immediate investigation of the massacre.[9] Mons. Pablo Vega, the Bishop of Juigalpa—perhaps the most erudite member of Nicaragua's church hierarchy—then responded to the issue of non-violence:

Here we have a very difficult problem, because certainly all non-violent measures try, of course, to generate a sensitive or moralizing conscience towards human demands. But when that respect (for human life) has been lost, our dedication to non-violence—which is the natural feeling of any people—is like preaching "Thou shalt not kill." At the same time, we have to add: but what if there are no other measures? For if someone attacks you, you have to defend yourself. Particularly in the case of an unjust aggression which is no longer an individual matter but one that arises from the constituted authority. Therefore, it is a very grave matter this practice of inciting the people to aggression or to initiating an aggressive defense in the face of institutionalized aggression.[10]

During Holy Week, 1979 (April 8-14), the people of Estelí took to the streets in a spontaneous protest against the regime. Once again the Guard bombed, burned and mercilessly "cleaned out" the city. As a result of the Estelí uprising another large group of Christian young people joined the FSLN in the mountains. Among them were 67 Catholics, 32 Pentecostals and 11 Baptists,[11] demonstrating the radical ecumenical unity created by the revolutionary process in Nicaragua. After victory these three sectors continued that ecumenical spirit by taking the leadership in the Marxist-Christian dialogue.

The church, like other social sectors, was inspired and moved by the poor and working class it was trying to serve. As Christians in city after city and throughout the country made their decision to help bring down the dictatorship, the question was no longer *if* they should do so, but only *how*. In defining their Christianity as a commitment to their people, they moved to increasingly higher levels of political involvement. The hierarchy had earlier acknowledged this as a legitimate and proper role for the faithful:

This popular reaction [to Somoza] has been interpreted by some as the product of foreign handiwork, based on strange ideologies. But "in its origin it is nothing more than the uncoercible cry of a people becoming conscious of their own reality and seeking to break the bonds that imprison them." This popular reaction is an expression of the will of the people and their patriotic demand which legitimately seeks its historic self-determination, affirming its national identity in the face of constant and permanent foreign intervention.[12]

"So, my brother, let us go forward. The march towards victory cannot be stopped and the hour of the ovens is approaching. Our role of burying the heart of the enemy is confirmed."
Modesto (FSLN commander)

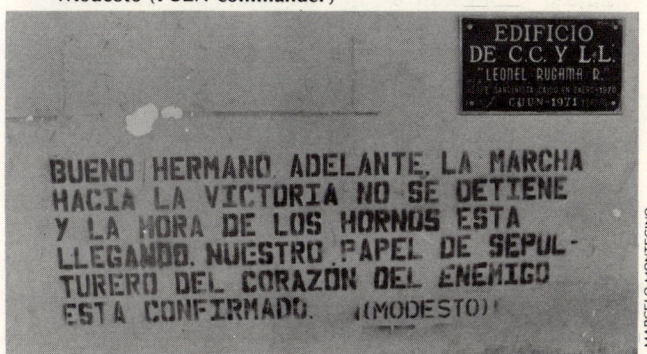

THE REUNIFICATION OF THE FLSN

"I am a city worker, as they say in this country, an artisan, but my ideal lies in the broad horizons of internationalism, in the right to be free and to demand justice, even though to accomplish that perfect state it may be necessary to shed one's own blood and the blood of others."
Augusto Cesar Sandino
July 1, 1927

The FLSN did not view its withdrawal before the National Guard in September as a defeat, but rather as a calculated tactical retreat. Nor did the Sandinistas hold that the results of the uprising disproved the efficacy of insurrection as a military tactic. They simply recognized that because the popular forces were unorganized and the "vanguard was fragmented,"[1] they could not take on the Guard until these deficiencies were overcome. As Giocondi Belli expressed it in the Fall of 1978:

> *The present situation calls for a tactical retreat in the military sense, to reorganize our forces, move to new forms of struggle, and unleash guerilla actions throughout the country. On the political plane, this is a time for offensive in order to qualitatively transform the enthusiasm and heroism (of the people) into popular organizing. By developing them militarily and politically, this process of organizing the masses is precisely the guarantee of triumph for the guerrilla movement.*[2]

The FSLN set about to seriously reorganize the masses using the MPU as its basic support structure. The September genocide by Somoza had made the people open to such discipline. The FSLN now knew that only all-out war could defeat the National Guard and that this would require the combined effort and organization of both people and vanguard.

At the same time, it was not enough to train the people; the FSLN itself had to be reunited. The person who spoke most clearly that Fall to the issue of unity was Bayardo Arce, who emphasized the importance of an integral relationship between the Sandinista vanguard and the people. This would require more than their previous "unity in action"; they would have to move to a higher level of coordination.

> *The situation continues to be a knotty problem, a problem that requires unity among our forces. We have greater difficulty untying this knot now because of the repression, since much of our work of organizing has been fragmented, particularly our work among the masses.*[3]

THE PROCESS OF UNIFICATION

During the months of October and November, the three tendencies held meetings to find a solution to their differences. The basis of unity had already been laid out in the writings and concepts of Augusto César Sandino. The programmatic heritage of Sandino contained seven basic points:

1. Establishment of a popular and independent government;
2. Cooperative management of the land to benefit those who work it;
3. Suppression of all reactionary treaties that have been forced upon the nation;
4. Integration of continental organizations that work for Central American interests, without Yankee or other foreign power involvement;
5. Recovery of our national riches and resources to benefit the great majority of our people;
6. Respect for our national values; and
7. Maintenance of a popular army.[4]

These points underscored a clearly anti-imperialist, class-oriented, nationalist and pro-regional platform that was as valid in 1978 as it had been in the years when Sandino developed them. It was on these points that all three tendencies based their unity. On December 7, 1978, "somewhere in Nicaragua" the GPP, Proletarian and Insurrectionalist tendencies drew up a "basis of unity." As they stated in their opening paragraph:

Six of the nine members of the reunified FSLN high command. Left to right: Jaime Wheelock, Daniel Ortega, Tomas Borge, Henry Ruiz,

[We] have decided to unite our political and military forces to assure that the heroic struggle of our people shall not be mocked by the machinations of Yankee imperialism and those sectors of the local bourgeoisie who have sold out on our country. We will unite our forces in order to advance the revolutionary armed struggle until the Somocista military dictatorship is definitively defeated and we have installed in our country an authentically democratic regime, one which guarantees national sovereignty and the socio-economic progress of our workers. This Sandinista unity which we hereby commit ourselves to reinforce more and more each day, will be the unquestionable guarantee of popular victory.

In this statement four issues of social progress and liberty are underscored:
- rejection of imperialism, its puppet Somoza, and any foreign intervention;
- rejection of any pacts or plebiscites aimed at betraying the aspirations of the people;
- the dismantling of the National Guard; and
- support of the MPU as expressing the people's "patriotic, national and democratic solution" to the present Somoza dictatorship.[5]

This initial unity apparently needed, however, more time to mature and had to be discussed with each tendency's broader constituency. The step taken in December was neither broadcast extensively nor was it *officially* signed. It is important to remember the extent of Somoza's repression under which both the Sandinistas and the people in general were operating during these months (December 1978-February 1979) as this unity was being consolidated.

Finally, on March 8, the three FSLN tendencies culminated their "program of national unity" which was signed by the "Joint National Leadership of the Sandinista Front of National Liberation (FSLN)":[6]

Thomás Borge, Daniel Ortega, Henry Ruiz, Humberto Ortega, Jaime Wheelock, Victor Tirado, Luis Carrió, Carlos Nuñez, Bayardo Arce

As this leadership said in their first editorial of *Unidad Sandinista* (the official organ of the FSLN for foreign readership):

Sandinista unity represents the maturation and synthesis of the revolutionary movement in Nicaragua. At the same time, it represents the accumulation of more formidable forces towards realizing the overthrow of the dictatorship.... Now the immediate task is that of generating an ever-deepening Sandinista unity. We have demonstrated that is is possible to have divergencies, and that it is possible to build our just cause through maturity and high values in spite of such differences. This example of Sandinismo *will surely be projected towards other sister movements which are facing the common enemy in different ways.*[7]

In the process of affirming their unity, the Sandinistas also further defined certain programmatic points they held to be fundamental for any future government. They would create a:

1. Provisional Government of National Unity;
2. Program of National Reconstruction;
3. National Army (without *Somocistas*);
4. Foreign Policy of Non-Alignment; and
5. Patrimony of National Reconstruction (that is, the expropriation of all of Somoza's holdings by the new Government.)[8]

This unification of the FSLN did not come easily, nor did it happen a moment too soon, given the imminent battles with the National Guard. Thus while the FSLN was overcoming its problems the dictatorship continued in crisis. The Sandinistas communicated the critical importance of this difference when they said in May 1979:

The fact that the Somoza military dictatorship and the opposition bourgeoisie have been unable to resolve their crisis because they could not eliminate the FSLN and the popular forces, and the fact that the FSLN and the popular forces have been able to maintain their legitimacy and popular support, and build sufficient force to defeat the dictatorship, and establish a Government of National Unity under the popular hegemony, gives this crisis the nature of a "revolutionary crisis."[9]

It is clear that this reunification of the FSLN was far more than an ideological consensus or an agreement about strategy. It was a unity forged out of historical necessity—out of the vanguard's commitment not to itself but to the Nicaraguan people.

Victor Tirado, Humberto Ortega.

PREPARATIONS FOR THE FINAL OFFENSIVE

Central Focus of Sandinista Strategy: Popular Insurrection

The uniqueness of the Sandinista strategy sprang from the dynamic unity which had developed between the FSLN vanguard and the popular forces. How would this unity spell itself out in an all-out offensive against the highly-trained, better equipped National Guard which outnumbered the Sandinistas ten-to-one? The FSLN saw triumph or failure resting not on its own forces but on the inexhaustible force represented by the people in opposition to Somoza. FSLN Commander Humberto Ortega delineated this understanding in a post-victory interview:

It is very difficult to take power without combining all forms of struggle wherever these can develop: countryside, city, barrio, and mountains. The struggle always revolves around the concept that the active masses are the central focus, not one where the vanguard is the central force, nor one where the masses are only considered to be a support force for the vanguard....

The activity of the masses allowed the armed struggle to accumulate the forces which those same masses needed....

We operated in such a way that these masses could continue to move. For that reason they appeared to be isolated parts of a military plan when in fact they responded to a political-military strategy to keep up the pressure (on the National Guard) and to give the people oxygen, because only in that way was a military triumph possible. [1]

When Ortega was pressed about equal if not greater importance of such factors as firepower (and thus additional arms for the FSLN from outside Nicaragua) or the matter of international solidarity, the FSLN leader said that those issues had a great deal to do with *how long* Somoza or the National Guard could hold out, and *how much* human and physical damage would befall Nicaragua and its people, but those factors would never in themselves guarantee the downfall of Somoza. Two things were crucial, he said: the unity of the vanguard, which "will continue to play a vital role in the revolution," [2] and the will of the people "to turn out into the streets and to do battle with whatever they had." [3]

Spring Diversionary Attacks: El Jíbaro, Estelí and Nueva Guinea

Winter and early spring preparations were not limited to training, storage and communications. During March, for instance, the FSLN attacked Granada, Masaya, Diriamba and León, plus taking over the small town of Yalí for eight hours. In the same period, the vanguard assaulted numerous banks where it "recovered" money for purchasing arms and sabotaged $1.5 million worth of cotton—20% of Nicaragua's harvest. Similarly, private school and university strikes continued with educational protests against ongoing repression of students by the BECATS. [4]

After FLSN reunification, the Sandinistas carried out their first joint guerilla operation by taking over the small town of El Jíbaro in the northern province of Nueva Segovia (where Sandino's army had been based). This attack in late March officially marked the beginning of the pre-offensive period, though its purpose was strictly diversionary. Led by Commander German Pomares of the Northern Front, his column attacked and held the Guard outpost in order to draw more Guard troops farther north, into the mountain stronghold of the guerillas.

In April, the second united FSLN action took place on Estelí. The original plan had been to use the Carlos Fonseca Amador columns to keep the Gaurd off-balance by carrying out a series of hit-and-run assaults throughout the Estelí "zone." However, when guerilla patrols—largely of former *"muchachos"* from Estelí—made a strike against the city in order to collect weapons and supplies, the people unexpectedly rose up as they had the previous September. When they had taken over the city they asked the Sandinistas to stay and support them. This popular initiative reflected the desperate and repressive situation in that area (Estelí and La Trinidad) which was so extreme that the people couldn't wait for the FSLN and ended up holding the city for seven days. The viciousness of the fighting drew other FSLN forces into the struggle until there were approximately 175 to 200 guerillas supporting the populace but encircled by some 2,000 Guardsmen. [5] In order to liberate those trapped inside the city, another column led by

Commander "René" drove through the Guard perimiter, opening up a space through which most of the guerillas escaped. Thus while the Estelí takeover was an isolated effort and not a signal to start the general offensive as some speculated, it did produce precisely the desired effect of drawing more Guard forces into the Northern region.

Similarly, at the opposite end of the country along the Costa Rican border, the FSLN was also preoccupied with the heavy concentration of some 3,000 Guard troops and therefore decided to open up yet another front as a diversionary tactic. The locale for this action was the small town of Nueva Guinea, situated in the sparsely populated province of Zelaya, east of Lake Nicaragua. In late April, with some 140 guerillas, the Sandinistas hoped to surprise the lightly defended town, but they were spotted before they could get into position and trapped in open country without cover. The result was a massacre of 80% of the FSLN column by some 1,000 air and land troops diverted from southern Nicaragua. This military setback was, nonetheless, considered a political victory because it fired the imagination of the Nicaraguan people to realize that the FSLN could move its troops virtually at will into an entirely new area of the country.

May: The Conditions for the Final Offensive are Fulfilled

The time for the FSLN to launch its final offensive was drawing near, but it had to await for certain strategic conditions, the main one being the economic crisis. Nicaragua's economy degenerated during the spring, with the loan from the International Monetary Fund representing the final blow. Somoza's requests for additional loans from the IMF brought to Managua in April an official inspection team which recommended that Somoza self-impose a 40% devaluation of the *Córdoba* as a pre-condition for the loan. The Central Bank complied, creating economic trauma throughout the entire nation. By May, commercial sales plummeted. As prices skyrocketed, the limited salary adjustments made by Somoza to compensate middle class government employees was no more than a token while the lower classes received nothing. By the time Somoza returned from his hurried trip to the United States, he had alienated himself from most of the Nicaraguan bourgeosie. As one FAO representative put it, "the country is a deadend; a street without any exit."[6]

In the political realm, opposition to the regime was also rapidly rising to the south as Venezuela, Costa Rica and Panama broke off all relations with Somoza. Costa Rica in particular was afraid that the expected offensive would only increase the use of its territory by Sandinista guerillas or lead to direct intervention by the Nicaraguan dictator. It is a fact that the Sandinistas were using Costa Rica as one of their bases of operations. That government half-heartedly attempted to clear out some Sandinista camps along the border (through a Costa Rican militia effort called "Operation Checkmate"[7]) in order to reduce this danger. This failed, however, because a number of large landowners secretly housed the Sandinistas as protection against Somoza's National Guard and because of the wide Costa Rican popular support for the FSLN.

As the time for the final offensive drew near, the FSLN had to integrate its three forces—a national strike, popular insurrection and military attacks—into a single strategy. Each of these forces had been used before, but never all three at the same time. The problem was one of coordination. To resolve this difficulty, a communications network was set up between the rural guerillas and the urban militia, between the MPU and the Civilian Defense Committees, and between the FSLN high command and the people. This last link was carried out through use of *Radio Sandino*, which had been functioning on a rudimentary basis since the previous March, but by May had become much more effective:

We managed to count on Radio Sandino *as the principal agitational instrument we had to guide both the insurrection and the strike. Without this means of communication we could not have triumphed, because we would not have been able to coordinate the war politically and militarily.* [8]

By mid-May "everyone (in the FSLN) agreed that the offensive should begin in the north; there was also a consensus about the need for a general insurrection." [9] Once again, the goal was to disperse the National Guard forces as much as possible. The place chosen to make this final attack of the pre-offensive period was Jinotega (north of Matagalpa). Jinotega was a critical area as the center of Nicaragua's coffee production and because it was a place which Somoza believed the FSLN had little popular support. the city was first attacked by the Oscar Turcios column of The Northern Front. At 5:00 a.m. on May 20, 100 guerillas led by Commander Germán Pomares overtook and held Jinotega for five days. [10] The success of the operation sent shockwaves through the National Guard. While only 19 guerillas were lost in this battle, the FSLN suffered a serious blow when one of its most respected and brilliant leaders, Commander Pomares, fell in battle.

Both Nueva Guinea and Jinotega proved to the FSLN that its columns by themselves could only wound the National Guard; they could not defeat it. Thus the high command now turned to its ace-in-the-hole—the so-called "Internal Front," the popular forces who would lead the urban insurrection. The guerilla columns had to regroup; they needed time to relocate and consolidate. Between the end of May and early June, everything would depend on the people:

The insurrection, as we saw it, would have to sustain itself at the national level for at least fifteen days, to give us a margin of time so the columns could regroup and then attack at an opportune moment. [11]

Sandino once said that only the workers and peasants would continue in the struggle to the end. The popular nature of this evaluation held true. This new Sandinista army was made up of dedicated Nicaraguans from all walks of life.

PROVISIONAL GOVERNMENT: PREVENTING IMPERIALIST INTERVENTION

On June 16, the FSLN announced it had formed a Provisional Government of National Reconstruction which would begin governing as soon as it could move into a liberated city. The membership of the Provisional Government was the result of long months of FSLN negotiations with all opposition sectors. The five leaders named to the governing council or *junta* were Sergio Ramirez, representing the Group of Twelve; Alfonso Robelo, representing the Broad Opposition Front (FAO); Moises Hassan, representing the MPU; Daniel Ortega, representing the FSLN's joint national command; and Violeta Barrios de Camorro, widow of *La Prensa* editor Pedro Joaquin Chamorro.

The Provisional Government of National Reconstruction issued its first proclamation on June 18.

We have assumed the historical responsibility entrusted to us of heading the Government of National Reconstruction to restore freedom, justice, and democracy to our nation.... The FSLN, in keeping with its pledge to our people, has called together the various social and political sectors of the country to form this new government so that it may justly claim its representation of national unity. We announce that this government, constituted with the total support of the FSLN and of all other democratic forces irrevocably committed to the armed struggle against the dictator-

Sergio Ramirez

Daniel Ortega

ship will implement a plan for national reconstruction. ...The Government of National Reconstruction will focus its principal energies on organizing and stimulating popular participation in solving our gravest national problems; hunger, unemployment, malnutrition, illiteracy, housing—all of which are the legacy of 50 years of Somocismo.[1]

Once inside Nicaraguan territory the Provisional Government's first acts would be to expropriate the Somoza family's property and dissolve the National Guard—two decrees inspiring the hopes of the entire Nicaraguan society which hated the Somozas and the National Guard so deeply. The proclamation promised that all men in the National Guard ranks who promptly defected would be guaranteed their basic human rights, and called for diplomatic recognition from all democratic governments in Latin America and the world.

The FSLN timed the announcement of the Provisional Government to coincide with re-opening their Southern Front. The FSLN had been battling Somoza in Managua for two weeks, pulling large numbers of Guard forces into that area. Fearing a take-over of the capital city, Somoza could not immediately send reinforcements south. The FSLN announced it would take Rivas and then install the Provisional Government in that city.

The FSLN also timed their announcement to coincide with diplomatic moves by Latin American nations. Mexico, Panama, Costa Rica and Ecuador had broken diplomatic relations with Somoza by this time, and other Latin American nations would follow shortly. On June 16, the Andean Nations awarded the FSLN with "belligerent force" status precisely as the FSLN was announcing the formation of the Provisional Government.[2] According to the Geneva Accords, this recognition opened the way for military support and directly challenged Somoza's legitimacy.[3]

OAS Abandons Somoza

Losing international ground rapidly in June, Somoza turned to the Organization of American States (OAS) but found no support. On June 4, diplomats coldly dismissed a Nicaraguan request for OAS investigation at the Nicaraguan-Costa Rican border. Instead, they accused Somoza of trying to distract them from the reality of the crumbling regime. Somoza had become an embarrassment to even the most right-wing Latin American governments. On June 11 Somoza's foreign minister again called the diplomats together to accuse Cuba and Panama of gun running to the Sandinistas. A group of activist Nicaraguan exiles in Washington, D.C. interrupted the session and astonished the delegation. They gave brief, impassioned analyses of the struggle from their people's perspective and expressed unwavering support for the FSLN and the MPU.[4] Following the unprecedented speeches, a foreign minister proclaimed that for the first time in OAS history it had heard the voice of the Nicaraguan people.

The decisive OAS deliberation began when the United States realised it had to take drastic measures or shortly witness an FSLN victory. The FSLN's announcement of the Provisional Government was only days old, when the State Department called an emergency OAS meeting and brought

Violeta Chamorro

a six point proposal before the body. The June 21 proposal did finally call for Somoza's resignation, but its major point of contention proposed that an inter-American peace keeping force be sent to Nicaragua.

The fact that the U.S. was clearly seeking to prevent an FSLN victory did not anger some Latin American members nearly so much as did the United States' manipulation of the OAS towards its own ends. They remembered all too well the U.S.'s 1965 Dominican Republic invasion under cover of the OAS. Not one of the other members supported the U.S. Completely ignoring the U.S. proposal, Panama announced diplomatic recognition of the Provisional Government. The United States' proposal cuttingly ignored the existing Provisional Government and called on the OAS to establish instead a government of "national reconciliation."[5]

On June 22, Venezuela and 12 other Latin American nations presented a counter-proposal having very little resemblance to the U.S. proposal. Most conspicuously, the reference to a peace-keeping force was deleted, and the wording strongly favored the FSLN. The Venezuela resolution passed on June 23—the U.S. having dropped its own proposal and joined the majority—with a vote of 17-2. It was an unprecedented defeat for the United States in the OAS.[6]

Meddling U.S. Diplomats

The United States did not, however, cease intervention. The State Department realized that if it were to have any leverage in yet another mediation, it needed to ensure Somoza's resignation. Accordingly, U.S. ambassador Pezzullo began negotiating a resignation with Somoza, but refused to make contact with the Provisional Government in Costa Rica.[7] The State Department spoke in its usual diplomatic doubletalk, "The political forces represented in the announced provisional government clearly would play a role in developing the eventual political solution."[8] The Junta members angrily denounced this position stating that the U.S. could not truly be concerned for rapid resolution of the conflict yet express no interest in contacting them.

The State Department drew up a plan aimed at negotiating a cease-fire and establishing a governing junta to rival the Provisional Government. The rival junta plan sought to minimize FSLN power by broadening the coalition to include two forces completely unacceptable to the Nicaraguan people: Somoza's Independent Liberal Party and a "cleansed" National Guard. The U.S. even tried to convince the more moderate groups represented in the Provisional Government to abandon it and join a rival junta. Both the Provisional Government and conservative opposition groups charged the U.S. with attempting to subvert the Nicaraguan unity.

These maneuvers collapsed on June 27 when the Broad Opposition Front (FAO) and the Superior Council of Private Enterprise (COSEP)[9] endorsed the Provisional Government. Without the support of these two groups, the United States' rival junta plan was exposed for its true nature—a means of denying the FSLN a military victory and political power in a new government.

Following this failure, the U.S. next campaigned to enlarge the Provisional Government junta to include more moderate members. The names of at least five persons which the U.S. circulated were charactized as ranging from liberal to unapologetically reactionary.[10] Sergio Ramirez, of the junta, stated that if any Nicaraguan group felt it was not represented in the junta and wanted to make suggestions, of course the junta would talk to them, but the junta was not taking suggestions from U.S. imperialism.

The United States tried three other tactics before finally being forced to accept the Provisional Government's make-up. First it campaigned among the other Latin nations, particularly among the centrist Andean Pact group, to withdraw or condition their support for the junta until it included more moderate elements. Secondly, they promised massive economic aid to Nicaragua if the FSLN leadership were minimized. Thirdly, they began rumors of Cuban aid to the Sandinistas—a favorite Somoza line. When forced on this latter point, the State Department finally conceded it had no proof of a Cuban-Sandinista connection, and actually believed that Cuban involvement was considerably less than that of other Central American nations.[11]

By mid-June the consensus in most of Latin America was that the U.S. had "no understanding of Nicaraguan reality nor of the overwhelming popular support the Sandinistas have."[12] With its diplomatic ping-pong the United States was considered the single factor holding back a quick resolution of the war, and an FSLN victory over Somoza.

FINAL SANDINISTA OFFENSIVE AGAINST THE SOMOZA DYNASTY

The final Sandinista offensive to bring down the Somoza dynasty occurred in three distinct phases:

May 29-June 8—Attack on all Fronts; popular insurrection and general strike;

June 9-25—Battle of Managua; the Southern Front feint;

June 26-July 12—Taking of Carazo; consolidation of the northern cities.

In contrast to the spontaneous, haphazard nature of the September insurrection, the strategy of the final offensive was to attack on all fronts at once. These included the:

"*Carlos Fonseca Amador*" (*Northern*) *Front*, led by German Pomares (until May 20, Francisco Rivera (Ruben) and Elias Noguera (Rene);

"*Rigoberto López Pérez*" (*Western*) *Front*, led by Dora María Tellez and María Lourdes Jirón;

"*Ulises Tapia Roa*" (*Central*) *Front*, led by Carlos Nuñez, William Ramirez, and Joaquin Cuadra Lacayo;

"*Roberto Huembes*" (*Eastern*) *Front*, operating in the Carazo region;

"*Benjamin Zeledón*" (*Southern*) *Front*, led by Edén Pastora, Alvaro Ferre, Tirado Lopez, Javier Pichardo and Daniel Ortega; and

The "Internal Front," the MPU-CDCs in each city, especially in Managua, in coordination with the FSLN leaders.[1]

The FSLN signal to begin the final nationwide offensive was the assualt on the National Guard barracks, El Narango, in the southern part of Nicaragua. Given the reverses suffered by the Sandinistas in Nueva Guinea and Jinotega, this attack could not fail and it did not.[2]

Attack on All Fronts:
The Popular Insurrection and General Strike

The forces in the Northern Front first took Ocotal and the town of El Viejo, north of Estelí. Its main offensive, however, was aimed at taking Matagalpa, where some of the most vicious street-by-street fighting went on for weeks. When the National Guard sent 250 reinforcements they were ambushed by the Sandinistas.[3] This strategy began a crucial aspect of the offensive: the FSLN disrupted or took control of many of Nicaragua's roads and highways, hampering National Guard movements. By the end of the first week of fighting, the FSLN controlled 70% of Matagalpa.[4]

The Western Front was the most successful military offensive. The main forces entered León on June 2 and by June 4 had virtual control of Nicaragua's second largest city. Within a week the Sandinista forces—guerillas, popular militia and CDCs—had mobilized the entire city and population into a socialist-model community, distributing food and medicines on an equitable basis.[5] The FSLN controlled the highways leading in and out of León, making Guard movement along the whole northern Pacific coast extremely difficult. In its second thrust in the Western Front, while unable to take Chinandega, the Sandinistas did take and hold the nearby town of Chichigalpa, creating a constant threat to the Guard's hold on Chinandega.

The Central Front carried out tentative strikes against Granada and Diriamba but its main target was Masaya, once again with all-out popular support from the *barrio*, Monimbó, the earlier "flame of resistance." Although the civilians and Sandinistas failed to take Masaya, the fighting was so fierce that Somoza was forced to resort once again to regular and systematic aerial bombing of the city. In the face of this genocidal tactic, the struggle there became typical of the fighting in many cities during June and July: National Guard control by day, Sandinista control by night.[6]

The main strategy of the Southern Front offensive was to hold the large Guard contingent (2,000-3,000 troops) in the south to relieve pressure on the Masaya-Carazo region. The initial takeover of El Naranjo was not an isolated assault but a coordinated attack along the entire Southern Front. Three hundred Sandinistas hit 11 Guard bases simultaneously in such scattered places as Peñas Blancas, Sopoa, Colón, El

Ostinal, and San Juan del Sur.[7] The outnumbered FSLN forces in the South could only fight a guerilla "war of positions,"[8] at this time, temporarily taking and holding towns or using hit-and-run tactics.

Somoza's strategy for countering the FSLN June offensive grew out of his "successful" September counteroffensive. Unlike the South Vietnamese strategy of defending cities, Somoza sought to liquidate the rebels zone by zone through bombing and clean-up operations:

> [He] has said he plans to seal off all occupied towns until the rebels exhaust their supplies, repeating a tactic used successfully to crush the insurrection in September.[9]

The National Guard had beefed up its regular forces from 10,000 to 12,000 with an additional 5,000 special and paramilitary troops, for a total of 17,000 versus perhaps 1,500 lightly-armed FSLN guerilas—a ratio of ten to one.[10] Such superior troop numbers, plus air power and massive armaments suggested Somoza's strategy might work again. The vulnerability of this strategy, however, like that of the military regime in South Vietnam, was the extensiveness of the FSLN Nicaraguan "Tet offensive" which hit the National Guard everywhere at once.

On June 2, Radio Sandino called for a "mass insurrection throughout the country."[11] The Internal Front or popular insurrection forces responded immediately and effectively. Their total commitment and tight organization were key factors enabling the FSLN military units to move quickly into advantageous positions in León, Chichigalpa, Matagalpa and Masaya. In Managua, the main offensive of the Internal Front was civilian-based. Somoza reacted by imposing an 8:00 p.m. to 4:00 a.m. curfew in the capital:

> Once again one could see the interminable lines at supermarkets, banks and gas stations as a sign that the people were preparing for the final offensive that would end the hated Somoza dictatorship.[12]

On June 4, the FSLN ordered a general strike. Within two days the revolt was more than 90% effective.[13] Somoza immediately instituted a state of siege throughout Nicaragua, which meant arrest without warrant, detention without charge, press censorship, and restriction of civilian movement. These actions paralyzed the economy and turned the entire country into a war zone. The FSLN now issued War Communique Number One, claiming Sandinista control of León, Matagalpa and Chichigalpa.[14]

In Managua everything was quiet. National Guardsmen and BECATs moved through the streets on cautious patrol; barricades went up or bricks were carefully set aside for that purpose. In many *barrios*, Somoza moved the curfew to 7:00 p.m. Government officials moved their offices to the protection of the Intercontinental Hotel. Guerrillas silently slipped into the city at night. The battle of Managua was about to begin.[15]

The Battle of Managua: The Southern Front Feint

The battle for Managua flowed directly from the victories and stalemate of the "four fronts offensive" and led to the consolidation of Masaya and Diriamba later that month. The FSLN's strategy in this struggle was aimed at winning time rather than holding territory, keeping Guard troops tied down in the city while wearing down Somoza's resistance and credibility. The FSLN made the capital city a front-line battle zone and thus exposed the war to the foreign press and international community.

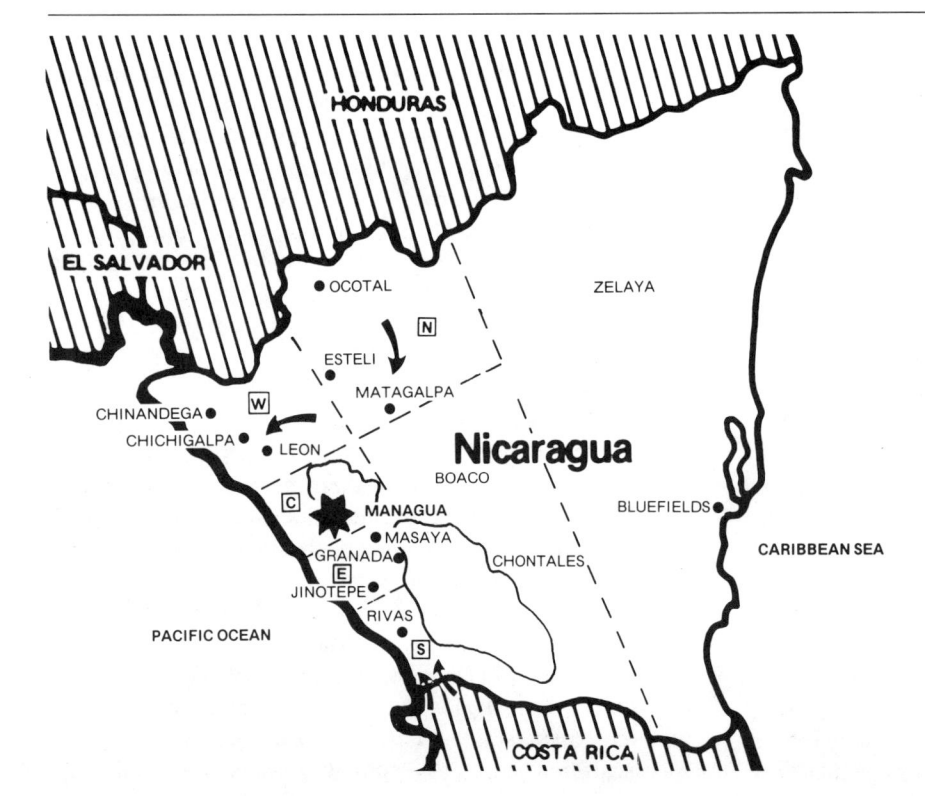

Final Offensive (Stage 1)

Roughly speaking, the five fronts were divided as indicated:

N - Northern Front (Matagalpa, Esteli and Ocotal).

W - Western Front (Leon, Chinandega and Chichigalpa).

C - Central Front (Managua).

E - Eastern Front (Masaya, Granada, diriamba and Jinotepe).

S - Southern Front (Rivas and Penas Blancas).

In the first stage of the final offensive, Leon and Chichigalpa were taken on June 2—4; Matagalpa was significantly controlled and the Southern Front attacked all along the border. By June 9, the battle of Managua began.

In addition, there were significant insurrections in Chinandega, Masaya and Rivas. Only occasional battle occurred in the Boaco and Chontales regions.

In the midst of the national strike, the Sandinistas controlled one fourth of Managua's streets, houses, stores and supply centers, literally closing down the city. Starting on June 9, the guerrillas, militia and *muchachos* simply took over, especially at night: They built barricades, ambushed Guard troops, and engaged the enemy in what the press called "fire fights," small arms shots versus automatic weapon bursts that were heard continuously until the victory. One poor woman described the mood: "For me the nights are a horror."[16] Terrorized by shooting, house-to-house searches and the regular disappearance of young people—girls as well as boys—many of whom were never seen again, few persons ventured into the streets after dark.

The Managua insurrection was no hit and run attack. The Sandinistas held the city captive for seventeen days and nights. Many poor and middle-class sections were completely controlled by the pro-FSLN forces. When National Guard or BECAT patrols attempted to enter and retake a liberated zone, they were ambushed. Barricades dismantled during the day were rebuilt by the following morning.[17] The Sandinistas blocked the road to the airport, halted the movement of trucks and buses, and forced most of the population to stay at home. Somoza sent his son to the United States to buy more armaments and airplanes, and he imported mercenaries from Honduras, El Salvador, Guatemala and right-wing Vietnam.[18] The United States finally evacuated most of its embassy personnel.[19]

The extremity of these conditions—including scarcity of food, water and other supplies—produced widespread looting and hordes of refugees. The society began to unravel from hunger and disease. Everyone was involved in the struggle whether they liked it or not. Looting became commonplace, and even took on a carnival-like atmosphere:

A giant warehouse owner, Constantino Campos, threw open his doors, allowing people to carry away 100-pound bags of corn meal, flour, coffee, and cocoa. Even the National Guard helped themselves to the goods.[20]

Money could no longer buy food. It could scarcely buy a way out of the country; a taxi ride to the airport cost $100. Somoza now admitted that Managua had been closed down.[21] As he had done during the past September, the dictator resumed bombing the FSLN's liberated zones and "people's areas." This resulted in thousands of new refugees: 50,000 from Managua alone. The situation, said the Nicaraguan Red Cross, was worse than the 1972 earthquake—worse even than Biafra.[22]

The by-products of the battle of Managua were crucial to the final outcome; the Sandinistas were winning "hearts and minds" while the Somocistas were destroying "bodies and buildings." By June 18, the new provisional government council was officially formed; the Andean nations—Venezuela, Colombia, Ecuador, Peru, and Bolivia—formally recognized the FSLN as a "legitimate army."[23] Meanwhile, the National Guard had ceased taking prisoners; they began shooting civilian suspects on sight.[24]

Ironically, Somoza's final *coup de grace* was inflicted by his own National Guard. On June 21, at a Managua check point, a soldier shot at point blank range ABC correspondent Bill Stewart. Somoza promised the United States a full investigation and pleaded, "I ask you to understand... that I never wanted (this) to happen."[25] However, the National Guard already had its orders to shoot all suspects on sight. The night before Stewart was shot Somoza had attacked the foreign reporters accusing them of being communist sympathizers. The execution of Bill Stewart captured on film by the ABC crew shocked the U.S. public, but it was merely one more example of Somoza's rules of war: the systematic killing of anyone deemed a threat to his regime.

Unfortunately for the United States, the Stewart execution occurred precisely as the State Department was trying to convince the Organization of American States to authorize an Inter-American peace-keeping force to "stabilize" the situation in Nicaragua. Secretary of State Cyrus Vance's June 22 proposal received the coldest shoulder the United States had felt from the OAS in decades.[26] The proposal included a belated condemnation of Somoza—an historic reversal of U.S. foreign policy—which was overwhelmingly supported by the Pan American Union, but the statement was little more than a polite condemnation of the long years of U.S.-Somoza alliance.

Cynical and undaunted by this hemispheric rejection, Somoza called for continued fighting to cleanse Managua of all Sandinistas. During the next few days, he napalmed FSLN-held zones of the capital. Symbolic of his megalomaniacal ego, the 1,600-man Guard force sent to eliminate the insurgents was called the "Somoza Batallion."

However, having accomplished their mission in Managua, the Sandinistas vanished under cover of darkness. Their tactical retreat towards Masaya, which took only two days (June 25-27), involved some 5,000-6,000 persons (guerrillas, militia, *muchachos* and civilians) with only 2-3 dozen persons lost in the process.[27]

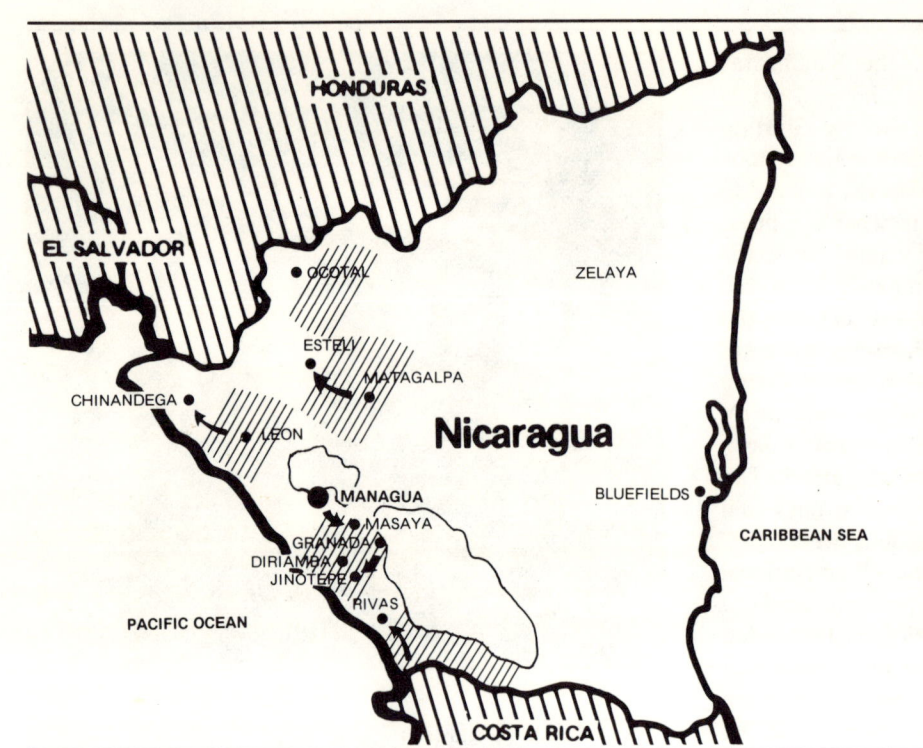

Final Offensive (Stage 2)

The consolidation phase (June 25—July 10) involved most importantly the massive tactical retreat by Sandinistas and civilians from Managua to Masaya which in a short time led to the consolidation of that region (called Carazo, that is, Diriamba and Jinotepe). By July 10, Matagalpa being secured began its drive towards Esteli and the Leon forces took over Chinandega. At the same time, the forces from the south were consolidating their hold and moving north towards Rivas. By July 10, the retaking of Managua was simply a matter of time.

Shaded areas show the greatest strength of the FSLN forces, not the only areas in which they were operating.

Taking Carazo: The Consolidation of the Northern Cities

The Managua strategy had worked: the Sandinistas left with overwhelming popular and international support while Somoza and his Guard were left with ashes and worldwide condemnation. The FSLN transformed their withdrawal from Managua into another victory. On June 25-27 they consolidated control over Masaya and Diriamba, where they now clearly outnumbered the National Guard. Within a few days, the forces moved west to take control of Jinotepe; within a week they secured the entire Carazo region. This meant that the principal roads between Granada and Rivas—the last Guard strongholds in the south—were cut, threatening the retreat of the Somoza forces back to

Managua. Retaking Managua had also been extremely costly for Somoza's northern forces; by now the Guard was unable to supply relief forces to the field:

> *The National Guard has been weakened (in the countryside) by wide-ranging guerrilla attacks. With heavy government troop concentrations in Managua, commanders were aware that outnumbered posts outside the capital often are left to fend for themselves.*[28]

These wide-ranging attacks shattered Somoza's strategy of controlling the rural zones; many Guard units were forced to concentrate on the Sandinista-held cities or were confined to their own barracks within liberated territory. The Somoza forces had become isolated islands within a sea of Sandinistas. Even where the Guard's superior firepower allowed their free movement in the countryside, the FSLN had almost total support from the peasants.

One Sandinista commander recounted how his brigade of some 100 guerrillas met 200 *campesinos* who wanted to help. The appreciative commander resisted the offer, not wanting to hamper his troops with unarmed, untrained farmers. The *campesinos* smiled and pointed to their shovels, hoes and machetes and said they would save the combatants, not slow them down. So they did. By dividing into teams of 2 *campesinos* to every guerrilla the FSLN forces were able to move across the relatively flat, open ground; when attacked, the *campesinos* would dig trenches while the guerrillas defended the peasants with return fire. This kind of alliance offset the technical advantage of the Guard's greater fire power.[29]

At the same time the Guard troops within the semi-liberated cities were becoming increasingly desperate:

> *A hysterical commander from the guerrilla-beseiged National Guard garrison in Matagalpa broke security and pleaded...over the radio for reinforcements. I beg you, I beseech you," he cried to headquarters, "Don't tell me they're coming [reinforcements] if they're not." From Diriamba, a town 30 miles south (of Managua), a commander threatened to "talk turkey" with the Sandinistas if government support did not arrive.*[30]

By early July, the FSLN began to consolidate its hold on Chinandega and Somotillo in the West, on Ocotal and Esteli in the North, and on Granada and Rivas in the South. Matagalpa was already liberated, and the Carazo region was the scene of heavy fighting. Somoza vented his rage on everyone: fleeing civilians, Sandinista *muchachos*, liberal sympathizers and conservative industrialists. The generally chaotic situation in Nicaragua became an apocalyptic madness as Somoza ordered his troops to execute civilians and his airforce to bomb rebel cities indiscriminately.

Ignoring the handwriting on the wall, the United States refused to break ties with the dictatorship and the new provisional government, thereby prolonging the massacres and destruction of the last days of the Somoza regime. The U.S. continued to act as the dictatorship's ally and protector. Its embassy in Managua granted hundreds of U.S. visas to *somocistas* during these last days so they could escape to the United States and thus avoid possible military tribunals by the new government. The State Department witheld recognition of the Sandinista *junta* while lobbying to get moderates who were more acceptable to the United States. Miguel D'Escoto, foreign minister for the provisional government, protested vigorously:

> *It is really a shame the United States [has] never shown as much solicitude for the entire population of Nicaragua so mercilessly slaughtered by the army it trained and equipped....Right now, the United States is the only impediment in the Americas to an early resolution of the Nicaraguan crisis. The transition of power in Nicaragua is the business of Nicaraguans, not of the United States.*[31]

The FSLN strategy of gradually wearing down the National Guard was now paying off. Of its original four Sherman tanks, the Guard now had only two. Of its original 40 British-made armoured vehicles, only 15 were now operative. By July, due to loss or mechanical problems, Somoza's airforce was at 50% of its original strength.[32] Meanwhile, the Sandinistas were recovering more and more automatic weapons and some sophisticated artillery along with trucks, mini-tanks and jeeps. The estimated numbers of disciplined fighting troops was becoming more equalized with the Guard. The FSLN numbered 1,000 in the south, 4,000-5,000 in the Carazo region, 2,000-3,000 or more in the North and at least 1,000 in Managua, for a total of nearly 10,000. The Guard was exhausted from lack of sleep and food; indeed, their glazed eyes pointed to their use of drugs to control rank-and-file defections. In contrast, the Sandinistas has virtually unquenchable reserve forces: the people.

By July 5, most of the city of Estelí was controlled by the Sandinistas. Chinandega was surrounded, Matagalpa had been evacuated by the National Guard and Rivas was under heavy attack.

One great resistance story came from Rivas. Pro-Sandinista forces held the center city, surrounded by some 1,000 Guard troops. The popular forces and CDCs were more concerned about aerial bombings than about enemy troops. They were particularly concerned about the 450 patients in the Rivas hospital, so they decided to evacuate. They led the patients out, single file, through the walls of the hospital, and then through one house after another, past the National guard to safety.[33] This escape was possible because the pro-Sandinista CDCs had prepared the buildings for such evacuations and because the Guard was completely isolated from the people.

By July 12, the war was virtually over. Radio Sandino announced that Leon, Chinandega, Esteli, Matagalpa, and Masaya were all liberated territory. At once the Sandinistas began to regroup their forces for their final drive on Managua. In the face of these FSLN victories, Somoza vainly attempted to mount counter-offensives, warning that he would shoot down any plane attempting to fly a "rebel government" into Nicaragua.[34] Time had run out for the dictator.

PEOPLE'S VICTORY, SOMOZA'S VENGEANCE

The FSLN's military victory over the National Guard was imminent by mid-July. Sandinistas controlled most key cities of Nicaragua except Managua. The National Guard, reeling on its feet from lack of sleep and food, was no longer fighting for Somoza but out of sheer terror for their own individual lives. Many small towns were following the example of Leon, electing local provisional civilian juntas who worked with Sandinista commanders to distribute the dwindling reserves of food and medicines. All were waiting for the dynasty to accept its fate.

The main impediment to decisive victory was the United States government. The only country to present demands to the Provisional Government, the United States, now limited these demands to safety for National Guardsmen, their incorporation into the new army, and free passage out of the country for any persons intent on leaving. The State Department believed that the Guard had to be retained to preserve order and prevent anarchy when Somoza went into exile. The FSLN knew the opposite to be true: the hated National Guard had to be abolished before the bloodshed would cease. No amount of U.S. pressure would force the Sandinista Junta to concede on this point.

The Provisional Government took several steps to consolidate its international support and quiet U.S. misgivings in order to hasten Somoza's exit. On June 28 it published a platform outlining the government's new organization. The Platform established a 33-member Council of State whose seats were divided among the FSLN, the National Patriotic Front, Broad Opposition Front, and the main businessmen's federation, COSEP. The Platform included declarations on fundamental civil liberties, human rights, dissolution of Somoza's power structures and repressive laws, organization of a new national army, and an independent foreign policy.[1]

On July 14 the junta announced 12 names of a proposed 18 member Cabinet.[2] The list included respected businessmen, religious leaders, a former National Guard officer, and FSLN leaders. Several joined the junta in Costa Rica to assist in drawing up a series of political, economic and social positions, and to speak to foreign diplomats and the international press.

The Provisional Government's "Plan to Achieve Peace," outlining an orderly transfer of power, was the document which finally received tacit U.S. approval.[3] The 4-step transition plan assured the Nicaraguan people of "the immediate and definitive replacement of the Somoza regime, already defeated by the heroic and combative people and vanguard."[4]

The Plan laid out the following scenario: Somoza resigns to his Congress; the Congress accepts and cedes power to the Government of National Reconstruction; the Government is installed and immediately receives recognition from the Andean countries; the new government carries out an 8-point decree which abolishes the Somoza constitution, dissolves the National Congress, and carries out a cease-fire between the National Guard and the FSLN. Safety of all National Guardsmen would be guaranteed so long as the terms of the transition plan were implemented.

The Andean nations immediately approved the plan, and agreed to witness the transition of power along with Archbishop Obando y Bravo and Red Cross Director Ismael Reyes.[5] The United States grudgingly approved the plan a few days later, holding its final ace tightly: Somoza's pledge to resign when the U.S. gave the signal.

While war raged on unabated, Managua began quiet preparations for Somoza's resignation. High-ranking Guard officers returned to Managua and packed their bags. All officers with 30 or more years of service were retired, an action which affected virtually every active duty general,

The people join FSLN leaders Eden Pastora, Tomas Borge, and

colonel and lieutenant.[6] This action gave those Government and National Guard officials time to empty the banks, coffers, stores and homes of any valuables they could find. Somoza made no public announcement of the Guard retirements, nor did he issue a cease-fire order to his National Guard. Shortly after midnight on the 16th, the Liberal party secretary announced Somoza's resignation to the waiting National Congress. Somoza, a few family members, and 100 Guard officers flew to Miami in a private jet shortly after 5:00 a.m. on July 17.

Somoza's congress elected Francisco Urcuyo Malianos, then President of the House of Deputies, as interim President. According to negotiations between the U.S. and Provisional Government, Urcuyo was to have only one function: relinquish power to the Provisional Government waiting in Costa Rica.

Whether instructed by Somoza or acting on his own

Bayardo Arce in a victory celebration in Matagalpa.

initiative, Urcuyo shocked the nation by announcing that he intended to serve out Somoza's presidential term until May 1981. He commanded the National Guard to continue fighting, called on "irregular forces" to disarm, and declared he wanted discussions with all democratic groups.[7] The delicately balanced cease-fire agreement was thrown into disarray. Junta members quickly cancelled a border meeting between the FSLN and the National Guard which would have opened cease-fire discussions.[8] The Sandinistas ordered the people not to lay down their weapons as the virtually leaderless National Guard began disintegrating in a blaze of random, terrorized gun fire. The weeks of U.S. efforts to subvert an FSLN military victory seemed wasted, as the Sandinistas announced they were heading for Managua.

The State Department, accused of deception by Latin American nations, withdrew its embassy personnel from Managua and called Somoza in Miami. Somoza blandly responded that as legally-elected president, Urcuyo was not double-crossing anyone, and that the OAS should intervene to "prevent a bloodbath."[9]

Early on the 18th, angry junta members Sergio Ramirez, Alfonso Robelo, and Violeta Chamorro, flew from Costa Rica to León. There they met a fourth junta member, Daniel Ortega, and declared León the provisional capital.[10] Upon hearing that the Sandinista government had entered Nicaraguan territory, outlying towns such as Somoto and Ocotal in the north, and Boaco southeast of Managua surrendered to the FSLN. Colonel Fajardo, Granada's commanding Guard, cursed Urcuyo for risking more National Guard lives in violating the agreement and surrendered Granada, Nicaragua's third largest city.[11] Hoards of individual Guardsmen began deserting, dressing in civilian clothing they wore under their uniforms. Many were shot by fellow Guardsmen to stop their desertion.[12] An incredulous opposition leader noted that the extended weeks of "fighting and...death have been to preserve this institution, the National Guard, and now it is falling apart in a matter of hours."[13]

Urcuyo's titular government lasted less than 48 hours. Unable to control the situation, he prepared to flee to Guatemala at noon on the 18th. However, newly appointed National Guard commander, Lt. Col. Federico Mejía was ready to negotiate with the Sandinistas, and would not let him leave. Negotiations between Mejía and the FSLN began, but not on the original cease-fire terms. Because of Urcuyo's betrayal, the FSLN demanded the Guard's unconditional surrender.[14] Sandinista emissary, Alberto de Palo Alto commanded Mejía to go on national television and radio and order the Guard to return to its barracks and accept Sandinista control.[15] Only then would the FSLN order its own troops to cease fire. Palo Alto promised that the FSLN would respect the National Guard lives and property if the terms were carried out.

July 18 was described as "the worst night of the 7-week fighting." Guard forces poured out their vengeance on liberated cities, looting and bombing them all night long and completely burning out some residential areas. In Managua and other cities individual Guardsmen, some not knowing the Guard had surrendered, others not heeding the call, battled fiercely without purpose.

By contrast, July 19 dawned on a liberated Nicaragua. Radio Sandino, moved from clandestine status in Costa Rica to Managua, woke the nation with Sandinista hymns and songs of triumph. The Sandinista broadcast called on everyone to "be calm, act with maturity. The moment is coming when all Nicaraguans...can go into the streets together and rejoice." The National Guard was told, "you have no reason to fight. Somoza is gone; Urcuyo is gone; Mejia and the entire command have gone. There is nothing to defend. Don't lose your life (unnecessarily). Go to the nearest church or Red Cross and surrender."[16]

The FSLN called on the CDCs to take charge, and keep order. They were instructed to maintain their Sandinista discipline, order and vigilance.[17]

As the joyous music and instructions continued into the day, people poured out into the streets. Truck loads of "muchachos" headed for Managua. Church bells rang in the border towns and refugees began crossing into *territorio libre*—free territory—proclaimed by signs at the border. The Junta left Leon and headed for Managua. Hundreds of thousands of ecstatic, tearful Nicaraguans gave them a thunderous welcome, gathering at the soon-to-be-named Plaza of the Revolution outside the National Palace. The Nicaraguan people confirmed in power the Government of National Reconstruction.

BARRICADA

FOOTNOTES

The National Patriotic Front: The People's Parallel Power Structure
1. FSLN, *Presencia Sandinista,* Monthly magazine of the FSLN's Committee of Exterior Relations, January 4, 1979, editorial.
2. Victor Sanabria Documentation Center, *Eighth Report on Human Rights in Nicaragua,* San Jose, Costa Rica, January 1979.
3. *La Nacion,* Costa Rica, January 26, 1979.
4. *L.A. Political Report,* London, Vol. XIII, No. 5 and *Eighth Report on Human Rights in Nicaragua.*
5. *Eighth Report on Human Rights in Nicaragua.*
6. *Eighth Report on Human Rights in Nicaragua.*
7. *Pensamiento Critico, Bloque Popular o Insureccion,* Managua, January-May, 1979. no. 3, p.20.
8. *Presencia Sandinista, p.1.*
9. *Pensamiento Critico,* p.19.
10. *Pensamiento Critico,* p.7.
11. *Pensamiento Critico,* p.18.
12. *Llamamiento Al Pueblo Nicaraguense.*
13. *Pensamiento Critico,* p.29.

Religious Mediation and Solidarity: the Role of the Church
1. United States Catholic Conference, *Report on the Situation of the Church (in Nicaragua),* Unpublished staff report following visit in September, p.6-7.
2. In Latin America, the term most commonly used to describe Protestants is *Evangelicals.*
3. See Dietrich Bonhoeffer, *Letters and Papers from Prison,* Macmillan and Co. New York, for the theological basis of Bonhoeffer's participation in a plot to kill Hitler.
4. Interview with Rev. Miguel Angel Torres, EPICA Staff, September, 1979.
5. Interview with Nicaraguan Christians by EPICA Staff, Washington, D.C., January 1980.
6. See "Business Work Stoppage & Popular Unrest." p. 20.
7. See *The Gospel in Solentiname,* Orbis Books, Maryknoll, NY 1976.
8. CONFER, "Nicaragua: Impacto de la Situacion Politica en las Tareas Pastorales y Sociales de la Iglesia," Managua, February 15, 1979.
9. Telegram, Leon, "Obispado de Leon a Somoza," February 15, 1979.
10. Interview with Mons. Pablo A. Vega, Bishop of Juigalpa, unpublished, mimeographed copy, February 22, 1979.
11. Interview with Rev. Miguel Angel Torres, EPICA Staff, September, 1979.
12. CONFER, Message of the Archbishop, Mons. Obando y Bravo, October 20, 1978.

The Reunification of the FSLN
1. Interview Henri Ruiz "Modesto," September 1978, "Asuntos Tomados De Entrevista," p.9.
2. Giocondi Belli, Dialogue with *Dialogo Social,* Panama, p.35.
3. Bayardo Arce, "Nicaragua en el camino hacia su liberacion," *Entrevista, FSLN,* pp.20-21.
4. *Ideario Sandinista,* Secretaria Nacional de Propaganda y Educacion, FSLN, p.5.
5. Comunicado del FSLN, December 7, 1978, "somewhere in Nicaragua."
6. Comunicado del FSLN.
7. *Unidad Sandinista,* Year 1, No. 1, Panama, June 1979, p.23.
8. *Unidad Sandinista,* p.1.
9. *Unidad Sandinista,* Panama, p.12.

Preparations for the Final Offensive
1. Marta Harnecker, "La Estrategia de la Victoria," *Bohemia,* December 1979, pp.4-19.
2. Harnecker, p.14.
3. Harnecker, p.16.
4. "Dios Une a Sandinoamerica," *Dialogo,* Guatemala, August-September 1979, pp.10,12.
5. EPICA interview, Nicaraguan Embassy personnel, Washington D.C., January 1980.
6. *Washington Star,* April 3, 1979.
7. *Washington Post,* April 5, 1979.
8. Harnecker, p.16.
9. Harnecker, p.11.
10. FSLN Estado Mayor del Frente Norte, "Communique," May 20, 1979. (mimeographed flyer)
11. Harnecker, p.15.

Provisional Government: Preventing Imperialist Intervention
1. Mimeographed, First Proclamation of the Provisional Government of National Reconstruction, somewhere in Nicaragua, June 18, 1979.
2. *New York Times,* June 18, 1979
3. *New York Times,* June 18, 1979
4. *Washington Star,* June 18, 1979
5. *Washington Star,* June 5, 1979
6. *Washington Star,* June 12, 1979
7. *New York Times,* June 23, 1979
8. *Washington Post,* June 24, 1979
9. *Washington Star,* June 26, 1979
10. *Washington Post,* June 19, 1979
11. *Christian Science Monitor,* June 27, 1979
12. *Washington Post,* June 26, 1979

Final Sandinista Offensive Against the Somoza Dynasty
1. EPICA interview, Nicaraguan Embassy personnel, Washington, D.C., January 1980.
2. Marta Harnecker, "La Estrategia de la Victoria," *Bohemia,* December 1979, p.12.
3. *Washington Star,* June 9, 1979.
4. *Washington Post,* June 7, 1979.
5. *Washington Post,* June 8, 1979.
6. EPICA interview, Masaya, September 1979.
7. EPICA interview, Rivas, September 1979.
8. *Harnecker, p.12.*
9. *New York Times,* June 10, 1979
10. *EPICA interview, Nicaraguan Embassy personnel.*
11. *Washington Post,* June 6, 1979.
12. *FSLN Bulletin,* June 2, 1979. (mimeographed flyer).
13. *Washington Post,* June 6, 1979.
14. *Washington Post,* June 7, 1979.
15. *Washington Post,* June 8 and 10, 1979.
16. *Washington Post,* June 9, 1979.
17. *New York Times,* June 10, 1979.
18. *The Guardian,* May 30-June 4, 1979.
19. *Washington Post,* June 13, 1979.
20. *Washington Post,* June 14, 1979.
21. *Washington Post,* June 14, 1979.
22. *Washington Star,* June 15, 1979.
23. *Washington Post,* June 19, 1979.
24. *In These Times,* June 20-26, 1979.
25. *Washington Post,* June 21, 1979.
26. *Washington Star,* June 22, 1979.
27. EPICA interview, Nicaraguan Embassy Personnel.
28. *Washington Post,* June 28, 1979
29. *EPICA interview, FLSN* Commander, Chinandega, September 1979
30. *Washington Post,* June 28, 1979.
31. *Washington Post,* July 4, 1979.
32. *Washington Post,* July 2, 1979.
33. *Washington Post,* July 4, 1979.
34. EPICA interview, municipal government members, Rivas, September 1979.

People's Victory, Somoza's Vengeance
1. *Platform of the Government of National Reconstruction,* Nicaragua, June 28, 1979.
2. *Washington Post,* July 21, 1979.
3. *Washington Post,* July 21, 1979.
4. *Plan of the Government of National Reconstruction to Achieve Peace,* Nicaragua, July 11, 1979.
5. *Washington Post,* July 17, 1979.
6. *Washington Post,* July 17, 1979.
7. *New York Times,* July 18, 1979.
8. *Washington Post,* July 18, 1979.
9. *Christian Science Monitor,* July 19, 1979.
10. *Washington Post,* July 18, 1979.
11. *Washington Post,* July 19, 1979.
12. *Washington Star,* July 19, 1979.
13. *Washington Post,* July 19, 1979.
14. *New York Times,* July 19, 1979.
15. *Washington Star,* July 19, 1979.
16. *Washington Post,* July 20, 1979.
17. "La Gran Victoria Sandinista," *Informativo Cencos,* Mexico, July 20, 1979, p.5.

74

QUE LA SANGRE DE NUESTROS MARTIRES NOS AHOGUE SI NO CUMPLIMOS CON SUS SAGRADOS IDEALES

May the blood of the martyrs drown us if we do not uphold their sacred ideals.

PART 3
LIBERATED NICARAGUA: August-December 1979

THE SOMOZA LEGACY: ECONOMIC BANKRUPTCY

Victory held a mixture of elation and suffering for the Nicaraguan people. They had paid an incredible price for their liberation: 40,000 dead—1.5% of the population, some 100,000 wounded, 40,000 children orphaned, 200,000 families left homeless, and 750,000 dependent on food assistance.[1] Without emergency international aid, the population faced imminent starvation. The major cities had been razed and the treasury systematically looted, leaving more than one third of the labor force out of work. But the legacy of Somoza encompassed far more than the war's death and destruction. He left them an infant mortality rate higher than India's and an illiteracy rate of 53.3%.[2] He left a deeply depressed economy; a neglected social service system grossly deficient in housing, health care, basic services and general urban infrastructure; and an insurmountable external debt totalling $1.5 billion. The cumulative effect of these factors meant that every sector of the economy was in a state of crisis.

Agricultural, Industrial and Social Impact

Agriculture, the base of the Nicaraguan economy, suffered severe setbacks because the fighting extended into the 1979 planting season. Virtually 70% of the country's main export—cotton—went unplanted, severely cutting potential foreign exchange earnings. Farmers missed planting the year's first crops of corn, beans and rice—Nicaragua's staple diet. The principal sugar mill was destroyed as the sugar cane became ready for harvest. The war interrupted a crucial blight control program for the coffee plants. These setbacks promised to severely affect Nicaragua for at least two years.[3]

Industry and commerce suffered the most from direct losses caused by the war.[4] The economy had ground to a halt three times in one-and-a-half years—in January 1978, September 1978, and finally during June and July 1979—paralyzing domestic demand. Somoza's aerial bombardment destroyed buildings, machines, and other equipment, totalling some 1,500 million *córdobas*.[5] More than one-third of the manufacturing plants located on Managua's northern highway were completely destroyed, and others suffered major damage; the Guard had systematically destroyed industrial areas in virtually every city.

This shoe shine box shall never again be the symbol of childhood. Year of Liberation.

Managua shoe repairman.

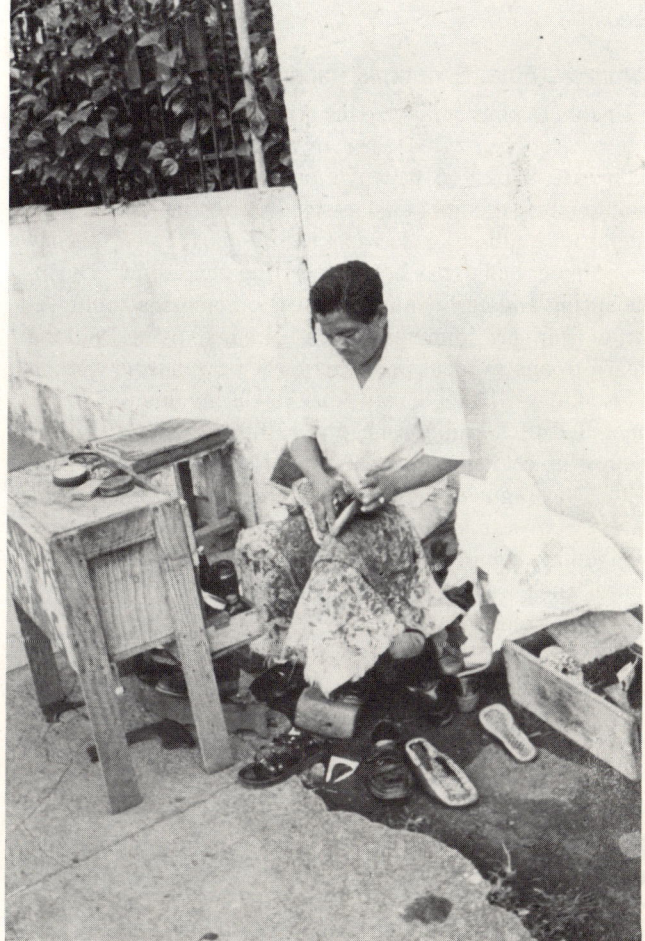

Somoza's legacy of bankruptcy to the industrial sector has an even longer history, its impact climaxing with the 1972 earthquake. Somoza's corruption and mismanagement of the reconstruction funds created a crisis of confidence in the industrial sector. Production stagnated; employment never regained its 1972 level in the same eight year period.[6] By the time of victory the industrial/manufacturing sector faced the future with a destroyed infrastructure, completely depleted inventories, uncollectable outstanding accounts, lack of raw materials, a drop in domestic demand—especially for non-essential goods—and a technical vacuum due to the exodus of many professionals. Initial estimates placed the reduction in commerce's gross product at 47%.[7]

Social services were also reeling under the impact of the war. Hospitals, schools, and housing had been hard hit in Somoza's "scorched earth" policy. The Rivas and Estelí hospitals lay in total ruin, while most others suffered partial physical damage and major loss of equipment totalling some 160 million *córdobas*.[8] Social services were totally inadequate for the needs of the wounded, malnourished, diseased, and psychologically traumatized persons requiring medical attention at the end of the war. The war caused a 15% decline in medical personnel; even before that loss there had been only 6.5 doctors for every 10,000 inhabitants.[9] Similarly, schools and housing—long neglected by Somoza and then ravaged by war—would require hundreds of thousands of dollars to meet the country's immediate needs.[10]

Somoza's Final Economic Rape: IMF Funds

Unable to physically take his private industries out of the country, Somoza came close to doing exactly that financially. He borrowed heavily from private foreign banks, double-mortgaged his businesses, left innumerable unpaid bills from multinational corporations—bills which the new government had to pay before receiving new credits. During the spring and early summer of 1979, Somoza slaughtered cattle from his immense ranch-holdings, using National Guard troops as meat processors when *campesino* workers refused to work. Illegal cattle exports during this war period amounted to 2.5 million head of cattle.[11] Somoza shipped the beef to cold storage in Miami for later sale, completely filling Nicaragua's 1979 beef quota to the United States before the war ended. Somoza's long-time allies also pillaged the country—stripping inventories from port warehouses and escaping with them in private boats to Honduras and El Savador.[12]

Somoza's final act of vengeance emptied Nicaragua's cash drawers of all but $3.5 million. He wrote last minute personal checks to himself and others totalling $169,000.[13] His final act of pillage involved the "disappearance" of $33.2 million, the first half of the International Monetary Fund (IMF) credit awarded Somoza in May, 1979. The IMF had granted Somoza a mixture of stand-by and compensatory loans on the basis of "economic" criteria established by an IMF delegation following its April, 1979 study of the Nicaraguan situation. Despite protests against the loan from renowned Nicaraguan economists, the entire Nicaraguan business community, and numerous U.S. organizations, the United States voted in favor of the credit to Somoza. The State Department feebly excused its position as one of "not opposing the loan." The IMF disclaimer that the decision was political was contradicted in a telegram issued by U.S. Treasury Secretary Blumenthal, arguing that such a loan could only be given assuming it would rejuvenate the Nicaraguan economy.[14] Since by May 1979, Somoza's economy was bankrupt and could not be revived under his leadership, the U.S. decision was obviously political in nature. The first half of the $66 million loan from the IMF was deposited in the Central Bank in Managua by June 1, 1979, and it was still there on June 9 when the bank closed down during the "Battle of Managua." But on July 20 when the second echelon officials returned, the money had disappeared, undoubtedly transferred to one of Somoza's foreign bank accounts.[15]

Tackling the Economic Problem

The Government of National Reconstruction faced staggering odds when it took power on July 19. Its broad goals were clear: strengthening self-determination, general economic recovery, and development of a truly democratic system. The *junta* realized, however, that it first had to feed the starving people, heal the wounded and the sick, and bury the dead. The task was formidable.

Somoza's $1.5 billion foreign debt was a heavy burden placed on the shoulders of the Nicaraguan people. FSLN commander Daniel Ortega stated before the United Nations General Assembly in September that the $600 million due on the 1979 debt could not be met:

It is our opinion that the external debt (that the Somoza regime) left in Nicaragua must be taken over internationally and above all, by the developed countries, the economically powerful nations, starting with those that routinely fed the Somoza regime. [16]

However, the *junta* needed to build credibility with the international banking system. It finally agreed to honor Somoza's debts with two exceptions: the outstanding military contracts between the governments of Argentina and Israel. These purchases of weapons, ammunition and aircraft totalled $7.3 million, with $5.2 million still outstanding. The government declared "Not one cent (of those bills) will be paid."[17]

The new government's economic plan outlined a new system to end decisively the past regime's exploitation and corruption which had left such a wide gap between rich and poor. Decree No. 3 of the Government of National Reconstruction expropriated all of the Somoza family's privately-owned or controlled businesses in Nicaragua.[18] In so doing, the state immediately became overseer of 50% of the arable land and 155 companies—representing one-third of the country's economic assets. The state also nationalized other key sectors such as banking and mining, thus enabling the state sector to serve as the principal manager of the new economic system.

Infrastructure for these state holdings, and particularly for the vast agricultural sector, would take time to build. In the meantime, the private sector must play a crucial role. It was encouraged to move into full production as quickly as possible. Recognizing that the private sector was as bankrupt as the rest of the nation, the *junta* nationalized the credit institutions to help steer private sector production towards the broader economic goals of the revolution. The government then immediately began to extend credit to small businesses and industries to facilitate their integration back into production. The *junta's* economic team outlined three guidelines for those receiving credit: generation of maximum employment, utilization of domestic raw materials and, minimization of any new foreign indebtedness.[19]

The preliminary "mixed economy" program which the government announced in July was meant only as a general outline of the economy's future direction. The country needed time to work through this crisis period, assess the reconstruction tasks and the stability of each sector of the economy, and calculate the possibilities for rescheduling the foreign debt and receiving international aid.

Given these economic parameters, the government drew up an "Emergency Economic and Reactivation Plan for 1980," which it presented publically the second week of December.[20] The plan described a "vital" role for the private sector, which would maintain ownership of 75% of the industrial sector and generate 60% of the GNP. However, the state's holdings at that time, particularly in

The remains of a street in Rivas, typical of much of Nicaragua's major cities. Residents search for anything salvageable.

agriculture and banking made the government Nicaragua's largest economic agency, indicating that the nationalized sector will be "vital" long after 1980's economic necessities have been resolved.

The revolution's overall goal was clear: to improve the standard of living and quality of life of the masses. This meant, among other things, a commitment to eradicate illiteracy, implement effective land reform, and provide free health care. The Sandinistas were determined to begin attaining those goals immediately. However, the desire to move rapidly and conclusively towards those ends was tempered by the circumstances of the past. The ongoing struggle for economic survival is perhaps the harshest price the Nicaraguan people will have to pay for their break from the old order.

SANDINISTA DEFENSE COMMITTEES: POPULAR POLITICAL BASE

During the last six weeks of the struggle the FSLN-initiated Civilian Defense Committees became the only functioning civilian structure. As the economy moved into its fifth, sixth, and seventh week of virtual shut-down, the CDCs operated a clandestine economy—feeding the *muchachos*, tending the wounded and setting up supply centers. When the FSLN liberated a city, the CDCs worked side by side with the Sandinistas, meeting the needs of the emergency situation.[1]

Victory brought momentary chaos. In the midst of the euphoria, people rushed about returning home, searching for family members and trying to comprehend the reality that 45 years of dictatorship were actually over. The old power structure was dismantled, creating a momentary political vacuum.[2] The Sandinistas immediately employed the CDCs to fill that vacuum and to perform the new tasks required in the rebuilding of free Nicaragua. The CDC structure remained intact, but to signify the new responsibilities, the FSLN renamed it the Sandinista Defense Committees (CDSs).

The CDSs had five newly-outlined tasks to coordinate: food, vigilance and defense, health and hygiene, medicine and distribution of information.

Food coordinators worked with the Red Cross, church and other emergency aid groups. They located grain and other staples, and determined where they were needed most. Many international agencies bringing in food relief distributed it through local CDS food coordinators. These coordinators organized meals for volunteer work crews—indeed for virtually the entire population—until mid-September, when the first salaries were available.

CDS health and hygiene coordinators worked closely with the Ministries of Health and Social Welfare. They located housing for those in their neighborhoods whose homes were demolished, brought severe cases of malnutrition to the attention of authorities, organized clean-up of areas which were breeding bacteria (such as stagnant water), and coordinated efforts to make fresh drinking water available.

The medicine coordinators identified the sick and wounded in their block who needed medical attention. These CDS workers checked for polio and malaria, the incidence of which had increased considerably during the last month of the war, and coordinated vaccinations of children when much-needed serums arrived. Early in September, the coordinators also worked with the Ministry of Social Welfare to locate all amputees so they could be sent to West Germany, where they would receive artificial limbs and rehabilitation.[3]

CDS vigilance and defense coordinators worked closely with *Sandinista* militia in defending the civilian population from the constant threat posed by renegade National Guardsmen. While many guardsmen returned to civilian life wanting to forget their past, others used illegal arms caches to seek vengeance, impersonating Sandinistas, or joining small night sniper groups. The vigilance coordinators organizing block security kept watch over suspicious persons, and guarded local meetings. A major task of the vigilance coordinators was to act as provisional judicial authorities until courts of justice could be reorganized and begin their work. All applieations for exit visas had to be processed through local CDS vigilance coordinators; no one left the country without a thorough review by their local CDS.[4] This minimized National Guard escapes and caught other *somocistas* trying to take their wealth out of the country.

The coordinators of information distribution (*propaganda*)* attempted to keep local neighborhoods up to date. New laws were being decreed daily. Step by step the country was returning to normal. As curfews were lifted, barricades dismantled, and other war-time restrictions removed, the *propaganda* coordinators made sure their block inhabitants knew about the changes. With the country's entire political structure being rebuilt, the FSLN needed a local forum to discuss and explain the decisions with the people. The *propaganda* coordinators set up meetings and circulated FSLN statements and declarations, functioning as a neighborhood newsletter.

The Sandinista Defense Committees were, in effect, the structural base from which the country began to dig itself out of the rubble and devastation of the past. CDS brigades took down street barricades and reconstructed streets, refurbished houses, hospitals, and other salvagable buildings, cleaned out the war's debris from the streets, and began the long process of cleaning away completely demolished buildings.[5] Because this CDS structure functioned from bottom-to-top, the coordination between blocks in each *barrio* was therefore effective at the city-wide level.

CDS Organization

The FSLN organized CDSs in every block of every neighborhood. The goal was to include the entire population in the process. Each local CDS elected a representative to sit on a zonal council. The number of zonal councils depended on the size of the *barrio*. Each CDS zonal council in turn elected a representative to the neighborhood CDS, called the Peoples' Committee. Each of these Committees (one to each *barrio*) selected a representative to sit on the city council, called the Peoples' Municipal Council.[6]

Local CDS concerns, suggestions and requests were thus shared with other committees, channelled to the proper authorities, coordinated with similar requests from other CDSs, and then integrated with the city's overall reconstruction and normalization plans.[7] Through the block committees, *barrio* committees petitioned for such things as increased public transportation to their area, a particular vaccination, or other specific needs such as a medical brigade.

The extent of the CDSs' responsibilities varied from city to city. Some cities' CDS municipal councils invited representatives of the ATC, trade unions, and other civic groups to sit on the council. In such circumstances, where the municipal councils included a broader representation, they actually took on a consultant role, serving as a mini-congress. The body deliberated on issues and brought them to the attention of the municipal *junta*. Guidance from the city councils in turn helped keep the *junta* accountable to the people.[8]

Despite efforts at local organizing and political education, many civilians unconsciously fell back into old patterns after the victory. In some towns, for example, in the first democratic elections for their CDS municipal council, the people elected the same *patrons* that had ruled for years under *somocismo*. Within a few weeks it became clear that these upper class individuals did not have any revolutionary orientation and were not fulfilling their tasks. To correct the old patterns, Sandinista leaders patiently explained that in revolutionary Nicaragua there were new criteria for those elected to office: skills developed by participating in the struggle and the desire to serve the people. In subsequent elections the people chose persons more qualified for the task. In some cases this meant a worker or old person who had no formal education was elected, coming to the position with a wisdom only the struggle could give.[9]

The Sandinista Defense Committees accomplished several important objectives during the first crucial months after victory. First, they pulled neighbors together to encourage common solutions to their problems and provided a natural forum for discussion and reflection on the country's rapidly changing events. Second, they integrated

80

virtually every citizen into the reconstruction process, keeping them personally involved in the short-term goals which the *Sandinistas* set before them and minimizing alienation from the rapid changes taking place. Finally, the CDSs carried out a new model of civilian work: a cooperative and collective process.[10] The experience of common struggle during the insurrection could not erase overnight the individualism and lack of confidence in leadership which 45 years of tyranny had taught the people. Under the dictatorship it had not been profitable to work together. Now it was an absolute necessity. Through the CDSs, the FSLN as the people's vanguard was fulfilling its promise to build an authentic, democratic popular power structure based on the workers and *campesinos*.

AGRARIAN REFORM: FOUNDATION OF THE REVOLUTION

The key to ascertaining the revolution's broadest goals lies in its program of agrarian reform, a long-standing Sandinista commitment to the *campesinos*. Decrees No. 3 and 38 issued by the Government of National Reconstruction provide the legal basis for the agrarian reform program. Those decrees expropriated all Somoza- and *somocista* owned lands and also made the following lands susceptible to future expropriation: those delinquent in payments to the state, those abandoned or controlled by absentee landlords, or those laying idle.[1] The state's new lands are referred to as property belonging to the people.[2]

Campesinos on an INRA-managed cotton farm in the Chinandega region.

The Somoza and *somocista* lands account for over 50% of the arable land of the country—most of it in export crops. With these lands the state now controls 20% of all agricultural production; as the state's underdeveloped land is brought into production, the INRA share will increase considerably. The state lands are being administered by the National Institute of Agrarian Reform (INRA). INRA is a department of the new Ministry of Agricultural Development (MIDA) which is responsible for guiding and assisting Nicaragua's entire agricultural sector toward the revolution's goals.

One of the important features of the agrarian reform program is that it is not based on breaking up large farms and distributing the land in small parcels to the peasantry. Instead, large farms will remain intact under state ownership, but they will produce for the benefit of the people as a whole and not for the wealthy few.[3] INRA recognizes that other attempts at agrarian reform have redistributed land to the peasantry only to have national production levels drop drastically, causing more hardship for the poor in the long run. Given Nicaragua's economic dependence on the agricultural sector and the need to bring in foreign exchange to re-build the country, a drop in production levels would severely hurt the revolution in its initial stage.

INRA is determined, however, that profits will not be

INRA approached its task with the best available resources. Under the direction of FSLN commander Jaime Wheelock, INRA developed an agrarian reform plan with three major thrusts: (1) *AGRO-INRA*, and (2) *Unidades Estatales*, comprised of the state-owned lands—approximately one million hectares in all (2.3 million acres)—and (3) *Pro Campo*, the program of services to the small-farm sector.

AGRO-INRA

The large state farms which have an industrial processing plant on site come under the responsibility of Agro-Inra. Because of the required investment in equipment and the specialized management and administration needed to maintain these highly industrialized and centralized farms, INRA has held large units intact and manages them directly.

Agro-Inra is organized by product. Rice mills, cattle and other livestock slaughterhouses, sugar cane and tobacco *beneficios*, and canning factories are the responsibility of Agro-Inra. Crops are organized in *empresas* (enterprises) which may include several farms along with the processing component. One rice *empresa*, for example, includes 22 farms. The *empresas* are INRA managed, with the workers salaries meeting the minimum wage law requirement. While INRA lacked the resources to increase wages during the fall of 1979, it sought to increase real income through social benefits. A Ministry of Agriculture goal is to provide free health care, educaiton, and housing on the state farms.[5] In the Masaya and Carazo regions, for example, some plantation barracks which were considered uninhabitable were burned, and new housing construction projects begun in September.[6]

Unidades Estatales

The large state farms with no key processing component are classified as *Unidades Estatales*, or State Entities. The majority of socialized land comes under this category. Many of the crops are the same ones which Agro-Inra manages, but these particular farms do not have the on-site processing. Without that direct link to industry they require a very different management.

The *Unidades Estatales* are organized geographically rather than along crop lines. They are divided regionally into state complexes (*complejos estatales*). Each *complejo* brings together the "production units" (referred to as U.P.s) or farms of the region, under a single accounting system. Profits are pooled and redistributed through the region on an egalitarian basis, in an effort to overcome the economic disparities of the past era. The U.P.s are run as state farms. Workers will elect representatives to work side by side with INRA in the U.P. and *complejo* management. The ATC is charged with developing worker leadership and management skills. The vast majority of the workers on the state farms in both Agro-Inra and the *Unidades Estatales* have joined the ATC. The ATC and INRA are working toward a relationship which expresses a partnership in

accumulated at the expense of the masses. Profits will be redistributed to increase wages, invest in social services, and invest in further agricultural development.[4] By thus utilizing profits from the agricultural sector INRA will improve the living conditions of *campesino* families and provide for future increases in production.

INRA's initial work of organizing and administering the state-owned lands was complicated by two factors. The most immediate problem was that the war had extended well into the planting season, and much of the land had not been planted. Preparation of a long term economic plan had to be balanced with the emergency situation. What little seed was available had to be planted immediately. Particularly crucial were cotton, representing next year's foreign exchange, and basic grains, next year's meals. In some instances, the *campesinos* came to the rescue. Understanding the emergency situation better than new management did, many peasants simply moved onto abandoned *somocista* estates or evicted the lingering *somocistas* and began cultivating the land.

The other complication facing INRA was the lack of accurate records on the extent of Somoza and *somocista* lands. Records were poor, "laundered," or most often, non-existent. Within a few months INRA had a fair accounting of farms in the Pacific region but a conclusive census of the state's property could not be completed by the end of 1979.

agricultural development rather than INRA being perceived as the boss.

Pro-Campo

The final sector services by INRA is that composed of small farms. The land in this division is either expropriated land that was under-utilized previously and has been turned over to peasants, or privately held land which peasants want to farm collectively. *Pro-Campo* differs from the other two INRA programs in that INRA provides services and agricultural advice, but is not responsible for the management of these lands. Basic grains, e.g., corn, beans, and rice, which form the basis of the Nicaraguan diet are the principal crops grown on these lands.

Pro-campo's task is to develop cooperatives which meet the needs of the small farmers. Thus far these are divided in two components. One, the service and credit cooperatives, offer technical advice and other agricultural inputs such as seed, fertilizer, and insecticides to the small farmers in each region. Farmers will have access to financial assistance and management advice through these voluntary credit cooperatives.

The second form of cooperative is the *sandinista* agricultural cooperative which is organized for production. Most of the land in the *sandinista* cooperatives was formerly small *somocista* farms or sharecropper land. INRA hopes that the peasants can quickly bring the lands into production for their own needs.

These lands technically remain in state ownership. *Campesino* families have been given 99-year leases and administer and manage the land on their own, enjoying the full profits from the farm.

INRA recognizes the need to be flexible to the needs of local situations. The *sandinista* cooperatives have therefore not been laid out in a hard and fast structure. On some farms taken over by peasants immediately following the victory, a "communal assembly" was formed as the authoritative body. The communal assembly elected a board of directors which included a director, secretary, and special directors for supplies, health, vigilance, education, and production.[7] Other tasks were assigned by the assembly as needed. A family is a full *sandinista* co-op member as long as it resides on the land. INRA seeks an optimum area of 5-6 hectares per family on the *sandinista* cooperatives.[8] *Excelsior* gave the following account of a cooperative in Leon in September:

> *The cooperative Jorge Barreto (formerly La Esperanza) used to belong to Oscar Galo, a close friend of Somoza. The cooperative was formed on July 27 and has 84 families. Twenty-five of the families live in the center of the hacienda, and the rest nearby. There are 700 arable hectares and 160 hectares which would be good for pasture but the cooperative has no livestock.... There is one fulltime agronomist on the farm. The cooperative has planted 350 hectares of sorghum, 162 hectares of corn, and 65 hectares of sesame. All of the families in the cooperative had previously worked...on the hacienda. Many of the members had participated in the insurrection. Most were illiterate.*[9]

The other type of land organized in the *sandinista* cooperatives is small plots of privately owned land which peasants want to farm cooperatively. The peasants are collectivizing their land holdings and combining their resources to rent equipment and sell their crop. The *sandinista* cooperatives are fewer in number than any of the other cooperatives, but INRA and the ATC together hope to convince other *campesinos* of the benefits in collective farming. INRA offers them assistance through the credit and service cooperatives, and other extension services of the Ministry of Agricultural Development. As of November, the ATC had helped form approximately 291 *sandinista* cooperatives with over 2400 members.[10]

Private Agricultural Sector

Eighty percent of agriculture's GDP is scheduled to come from the private sector in 1980.[11] Cotton, Nicaragua's major export, is largely produced by the private sector. The Government of National Reconstruction has guaranteed respect for private property. However, that guarantee is tempered by several important controls. One is a set of strictly enforced labor code standards. Peasants shall never again be forced to work under the oppression of the old era. Another control on the private sector is the nationalization of foreign trade.[12] The state will be the single purchasing agent of export crops and through pre-determined prices, the private sector will receive fair but strictly regulated profits.

The private sector will continue to be an important economic factor through 1980 while INRA is organizing and building its infrastructure, and putting the vast amounts of under or undeveloped land into production. A large part of that unexploited land is in the Atlantic coastal region—a region virtually ignored by the Somoza dictatorship. INRA is bringing that land into production and wants to encourage peasants to relocate in that area.

INRA is in an experimental stage, revising its structures and management to meet the needs of the people and economy. Many of its steps from July to December 1979 were preliminary actions to prepare for true agrarian reform.[13] INRA officials said in September that INRA had not really begun such reform; it had only retrieved the lands which rightfully belonged to the people and was in the process of sorting them out.[14] By early 1980, INRA had not just expropriated land; it had begun reorganizing worker participation and re-oriented profit distribution to benefit workers and the country's entire agricultural sector—all important steps in moving toward socialist agrarian relations.

LABOR ORGANIZING: THE ATC AND CST

The key to our victory and also the bridge from which we will move towards defending and deepening the revolution is the unity of the Sandinista vanguard with the entire population, but particularly with its most exploited sectors.[1]

This quote by the FSLN leadership appeared only a week after victory and reiterated the Sandinista's earlier commitment to the working class. The two primary organizations designated to carry out the goal of labor organizing are the Association of Rural Workers (ATC) and the urban-based Sandinista Workers Confederation (CST). The goal of both the ATC and CST is "to unite the fundamental interests of the workers."[2]

Association of Rural Workers (ATC)

Underlying all the tasks of the ATC is its main objective of reversing privatized attitudes towards agricultural production—educating workers about the critical importance of the collective goals of farming:

Traditionally, this sector of campesino *labor has worked for the benefit of the individual farmer. The ATC is now organizing our* campesinos *so that the history as a* modus vivendi *can be definitely wiped out.*[3]

This goal implies two fundamental tasks: first, to help *campesinos* manage and effectively develop the farms they now control, particularly the cooperatives; and second, to protect the rights of peasants working on privately owned farms. Towards these ends, labor congresses were held in

Workers and Campesinos to power. Frente Obrero office in Chinandega.

the fall of 1979 at which the *campesinos* discussed and approved ATC statutes and elected their own leadership.[4] A specific area of work assigned to the ATC is the vast Atlantic half of Nicaragua. There, the aim is first to organize and educate the hunters and fishermen—the traditional occupations of the region; and second, to cultivate those large tracts of land that for years have remained fallow and undeveloped.

During the early months of the revolution, traditional relationships and exploitation continued in the rural areas because there was an abundance of unemployed rural workers, and the private farmers had the equipment and capital to begin planting immediately. By contrast, the government had limited resources and therefore, even on the newly acquired state farms, workers were paid the same as before the revolution.[5] The result was that while the private owners pushed forward with their production they also paid low wages, i.e., about what the government paid.

This dynamic made ATC organizing of all *campesinos* extremely important. Although private property and private farming are expected to continue for a long time, such organizing will make it increasingly difficult for private landowners to exploit the abundant Nicaraguan labor force in the countryside. In the future, this organizing and its accompanying demands will limit labor exploitation and thus profit-making. Presumably, this will gradually force the private owner to either join the revolution or sell out.

The labor/production dynamic on the large plantations is

a somewhat different reality. Sugar mill workers, for example, represent a higher-skilled labor sector than the field hands, which means they should technically come under the jurisdiction of the CST. In the past labor organizing only took place at the plantation mill or packing houses. The new era in labor organizing found the lines between the ATC and CST overlapping, especially in this plantation sector of production.

During the Somoza regime, "white" or company unions (Nicaraguan or U.S.-affiliates) seldom challenged plantation owners or obtained many benefits for their members. Those plantations not expropriated by the new government were still exploiting their workers after victory. At the Standard Fruit banana plantation near Chinandega, for instance, men and women were working under extremely harsh and unsanitary conditions in the fall of 1979.[6] A labor struggle is already underway, however, as rural workers increasingly share their grievances with ATC representatives. As a result of this organizing, there were indications that Standard Fruit might pull out of Nicaragua, no doubt planning to compensate for their loss in Nicaragua by purchasing more bananas from their holdings in Honduras. This represents an on-going threat to the new government and points to the international implications of these new labor policies.

Sandinista Workers Confederation (CST)

The CST is by far the largest Nicaraguan labor body; as of September 1979 representing more than 90 trade unions. This includes carpenters, taxi and bus drivers, gasoline attendants, artisans and artists, woodcutters, bank workers, electricians and industrial and telecommunications employees.[7]

The CST is structurally independent of the FSLN, although the Sandinistas are clearly behind the Confederation as its support base and ideological mentor. This technical distinction is important not only because the CST includes many unions which previously had other political affiliations but also because the FSLN wants to assure both business interests and workers themselves that it is committed to free trade unionism. One thing is clear: the CST functions democratically, and workers and unions are joining it because their experience with the FSLN during the struggle convinced them that their interests will be more effectively served through the CST.

During the Somoza dynasty, there were three major labor

organizations: the Nicaraguan Workers Confederation (CTN), a social democratic group affiliated with the Latin American Workers Confederation (CLAT) based in Caracas; the General Labor Confederation (CGT) a Marxist-oriented confederation affiliated with the Permanent Congress of Trade Union Unity, based in Europe; and the Confederation of United Trade Unionists (CUS) a pro-capitalist union affiliated with ORIT (AFL-CIO) based in the United States. However,

> At no time did these labor organizations represent more than 8% of the workforce. Two of these organizations, the CTN and CGT, were identified as opposed to the (Somoza) regime and were forced to assume quasi-clandestine modes of operations. The CUS was permitted to operate (openly).[8]

The CUS had this freedom because Somoza knew the union would not participate in any political activities against his regime. Nevertheless, while claiming political neutrality, the CUS did join the Broad Opposition Front (FAO) in 1978. Under the radicalizing conditions in Nicaragua, however, this move implied a pro-*somocista* stance. For this reason, CUS had little credibility after victory. Thus today, when the anti-communist educational branch of the AFL-CIO—the American Institute for Free Labor Development (AIFLD)—disparages the CST as signifying the end of "free" trade unionism in Nicaragua,[9] it is in fact a reflection of CUS's organizing ineffectiveness and of AIFLD's reactionary politics.

One continuing labor conflict in Nicaragua today is that between the Sandinista unions (CST and ATC) and the social democratic unions (CTN-CLAT). The CTN, supported by monies from Venezuela and West Germany, moved quickly after the revolution to secure a stronger foothold in the country. CLAT's goal was to take advantage of the new freedom to organize provided by the new government. It held a Central American regional meeting in Managua in September, out of which it published a CLAT position paper which implied Sandinista domination of the trade union movement.[10] While the FSLN accepted CTN organizing as perfectly legitimate, it resented social democratic attacks on the CST and ATC. Nonetheless, the CTN organizing is proof that free trade unionism exists in Nicaragua, a fact which is being denied by AIFLD.

The real issue in the trade union movement in Nicaragua is not *freedom* but *class*. The Sandinistas clearly want to base the emerging new society on equality and justice for workers and peasants. The implication of this goal points to a challenge of management. In fact the new government hopes to win management over to its goals. Thus at a Managua labor seminar of the CST, Commander Carlos Núñez declared that it was important to distinguish between those members of the bourgeoisie who are still influenced by imperialism and those who had been victims of the dictatorship because, he said, the latter are individuals the FSLN "wants to attract and consolidate into the revolution."[11]

However, Núñez also reiterated the Sandinistas' primary commitment to the working class when he declared that one of the missions of the CST is to prepare the best sons and daughters of the revolution "to participate directly in the management of those industries confiscated from the *somocistas*."

Reconstruction of a Managua street which had been taken up for an urban barricade.

RISING SOCIAL & POLITICAL PROBLEMS

Poverty, unemployment and physical destruction were the basic causes of Nicaragua's social and political problems after victory. Although Nicaraguans had lived with these problems for years under Somoza, many people presumed that the revolution would resolve the difficulties overnight. Obviously, it could not. The new government was in a state of reorganization, lacking the infrastructure and resources to even begin resolving the more serious systemic problems. Thousands of Nicaraguans remained armed in protection against unyielding Guardsmen. Given all of these difficulties, it is amazing that the country did not explode into greater violence during the early months after Somoza was defeated.

In the face of these basic problems, the new government and its FSLN vanguard were caught in the predicament of wanting to establish order while demonstrating to its people and the world a climate of "political pluralism," a promise closely watched by the middle class and liberal press.

In no way can the decree [of reserving the term Sandinista for the FSLN] be interpreted as a negation of the ideological pluralism which is a "fundamental principle of the Nicaraguan revolution." [1]

Given the chaotic conditions in the country, however, this desire for ideological flexibility naturally gave certain license to extremist and opportunistic factions.

The ultra-left, ultra-right and middle-class opportunists created problems almost from the day of victory. The tendency of the press to confuse these political problems with the chaotic social life in Nicaragua at the time, makes it important to define each of these three political reactions to the Sandinista victory.

The Ultra-Left Reaction

The Simón Bolívar Brigade, which included Latin Americans from a number of countries, entered Nicaragua shortly after July 19. It immediately began to press the Government of National Reconstruction to take more radical steps to the left. It soon became apparent that the Brigade's political orientation was anarchistic. It urged a simplistic, rapid move to socialism, fearing that middle-class and reactionary elements would co-opt the revolution. Its members encour-

Workers and Campesinos challenge reactionary attitudes: "Anti-communism is equal to Somocismo."

aged factory workers to strike and *campesinos* to occupy land on farms belonging to the upper class, whether or not factory and landowners were *somocistas*. The new government faced the delicate problem of trying to initiate a progressive social program without any funds; if the new leadership moved as fast as the Brigade demanded they would likely be denied foreign loans. Because of this danger the government decided that the Brigade must leave the country.

A more serious expression of ultra-leftism came from a Nicaraguan organization called Workers Front (*Frente Obrero*). This Front, which had struggled hard against Somoza through its rural forces called the *Milpas*, argued that this was the moment for an all-out move to the left, using slogans such as "Socialism Now." Toward that end, armed *campesinos* began seizing the land that had been so long denied them. Although sympathetic to these demands, the government maintained that these forced take-overs of property threatened its step-by-step land return strategy. Tomás Borge spoke for the new regime: "The Revolution will act with a strong and firm hand, because it cannot allow counter-revolution in the name of Revolution."[2]

The Ultra-Right Reaction

Although *somocismo* was thoroughly discredited, conservative reactions to Somoza's defeat caused widespread social disruption. Almost immediately after victory *somocista* terrorists began nightly sniper attacks against civilians and Sandinistas in certain neighborhoods.

On September 24, Oscar Rivas Gallard, a 19-year-old Sandinista was killed by some para-military somocistas who had been attacking people in the Monseñor Lezcano barrio of Managua. When Oscar went out of the Sandinista Center, he was shot down by paramilitaries hiding in nearby cars. An old woman from the barrio said, "They were killing us before and they want to keep on killing us."

At the funeral on September 26, FSLN Commander Luis Carrión, visibly moved, said: "The Guardsmen fear the militia (of the Popular Sandinista Police) because even without training they showed the somocistas their courage.... This is a warning that the fight continues on a war footing, and we are not going to allow these vermin to keep on killing our young people."[3]

These isolated acts of vengeance or terror had no possibility of success; they only filled the population with hatred and fear.

Middle Class Opportunism

In the early days of the new government, many Nicaraguans who had remained peripheral to the struggle, quickly and easily declared themselves "Sandinista." A "Sandinista" barber or beauty shop[4] flying a red-and-black FSLN flag in an upper-class Managua neighborhood may sound amusing but such opportunism soon became a serious problem. The Christian Democratic Party (PDC), for example, decided to add the term *Sandinista* to its title. Even though its members had opposed Somoza, the party had never endorsed the FSLN and took only minimal risks during the dictatorship. To counter this tendency, on September 19 the government prohibited any political use of the term Sandinista except by FSLN organizations:

DECREE: Article I. The political use of the denomination "SANDINISTA" and its symbols and designations remain exclusively reserved for the SANDINISTA FRONT OF NATIONAL LIBERATION (FSLN) and the civic-labor groups and personnel integral to or under the direction of this organization.[5]

The Latin American Workers Confederation (CLAT) represented another form of opportunism. CLAT's regional meeting in Managua on September 20 declared that "Only The People Can Save The People" and called for "liberty and democracy" without mentioning either the FSLN or the Government of National Reconstruction. Using generic terms like "worker" and "peasant," the meeting's declaration said that the revolution was led "by all the Nicaraguan people, particularly the workers in the countryside and the city."[6] The statement even suggested that the change taking place in Nicaragua was merely an exchange of one leader for another, and "a change in bosses is not liberation."

These affronts to the revolutionary leadership, coupled with such opportunistic efforts, infuriated the new government. FSLN Commander Carlos Núñez rebuked the critics:

Groups called the "Social Democratic Sandinista Party" and Christian Sandinistas now say they defend the legacy of the General of Free Men, Augusto César Sandino. When they should have called themselves this they did not because they knew a bullet would be waiting for them if they had resisted during the struggle. We of the FSLN did not shrink before the bullets and crimes of the somocista regime....During his rule, the dictator said Sandino was a liberal and we were communists. Today, this Social Democratic Party is saying, "Sandinismo, Yes; Communism, No." But we are saying, "This Revolution is ours." The people will go with the FSLN to the end, to the ultimate consequences, because the FSLN is part of the people.[7]

The government and the FSLN reinforced the frequent condemnations of *somocismo*, ultra-leftism and opportunism. They delegated the Sandinista Defense Committees (CDSs) as the "eyes and ears of the Revolution against reactionary elements" in the society.[8] On July 30, the government set up "Emergency Tribunals" in local neighborhoods to deal with assansins. It also set down strict penalties for abuses: one to four years for acts of pillage, sacking, vandalism and destruction of property; and three to ten years for sabotage.[9]

The disruption caused by the ultra-right and ultra-left forced the government to increase discipline within FSLN ranks and to reorganize itself. The FSLN guerrilla army became the Sandinista Popular Army (EPS) and the militia became the Sandinista Police or the Popular Sandinista Militia (MPS). Those not officially designated as part of one of these forces were required to turn in their arms. During the fall of 1979, the society gradually returned to relative peace as the government, FSLN and various popular organizations were able to implement the order called for in such early slogans as "Organization and Discipline." One FSLN leader summarized the task of the new regime: "We have to act in a disciplined manner, because we can lose the freedom we have won with so much blood if we fall into anarchy.... Revolution means organization and the decision to defend it."[10]

POPULAR POLITICAL EDUCATION

The majority of Nicaraguans grasped the meaning of the end of the Somoza era more easily than they understood the implications of the Sandinista triumph. Recognizing that the society had yet to learn the goals of the revolution, the FSLN initiated numerous kinds of popular education during the fall of 1979. The three primary instruments of this politicization process used during the early months of the new era were: the burial of martyrs, political seminars, and the mass media.

Burial of Martyrs and Heroes

In the first months of revolutionary triumph, Nicaraguans marched in solemn processions, stood in somber meetings, and carried banners through their streets and neighborhoods memorializing the revolution's 40,000 martyrs and heroes. The FSLN and the new government used these memorial services for political education, pointing the people to a new day and a new hope. "They say that revolution is bitter; it is not. It's the sugar that will sweeten the bitter drinks of our history," wrote Morales Avilez, one hopeful Nicaraguan poet.[1]

In Matagalpa on August 1, Tómas Borge, Bayardo Arce and Edén Pastora of the FSLN high command marched with 3,000 others in tribute to one of the Sandinista founders, Carlos Fonseca Amador. At the memorial service in San José Church, the leaders declared Matagalpa a national sanctuary.[2] On the same day in Managua, the residents of *barrio* San Judas gathered to inaugurate a Gallery of Martyrs in honor of their martyred heroine Auro Lila Mendoza (Verónica), who helped found the CDCs and coordinate the MPU. As another poet reflected, "Our heroes did not *say* they would die for their country; they died for Nicaragua.[3]

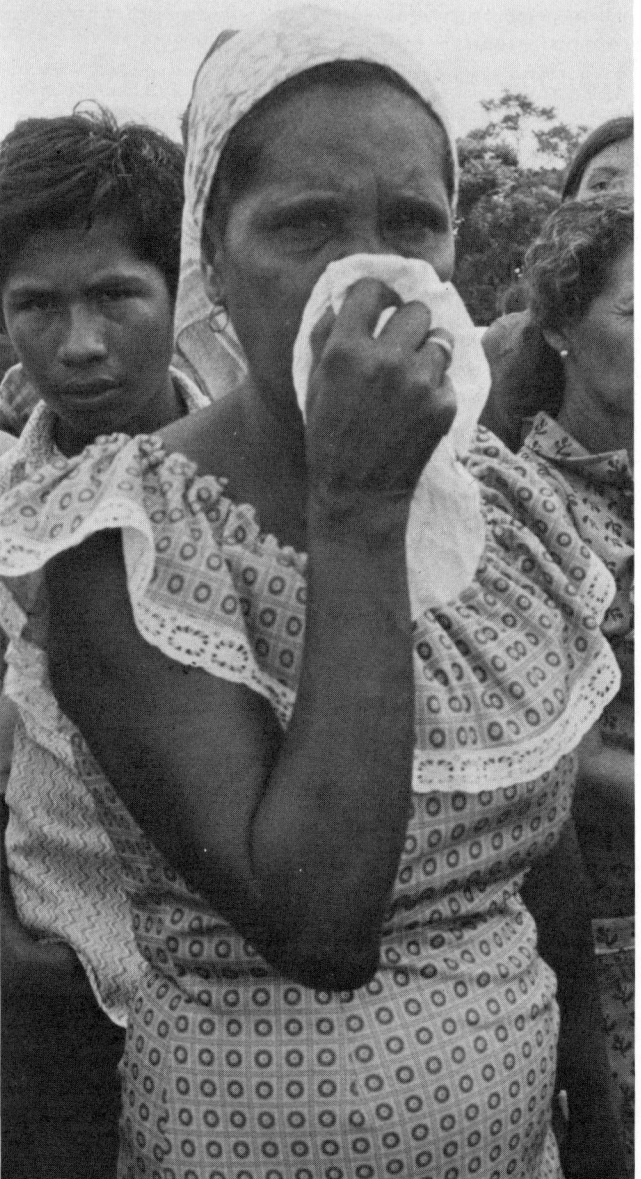

But the revolutionary leadership had to move the people beyond reflection on the past. On August 16, the great peasant leader Commander Germán Pomares Ordoñez was hailed as "a symbol of all the heroes of the revolution and above all a symbol of the most oppressed and exploited sectors of our country."[4] At his funeral, FSLN Commander Daniel Ortega Saavedra turned the eulogy from personal lament into political projection:

> We are not going to make this act a long one by remembering all the martyrs and heroes among the campesinos of the north of our country and their contribution against Somoza; we have come here to emphasize the need to invest all our effort, all our energy, all our capacity in the great task of national reconstruction.[5]

Political Education Seminars

Beyond these public memorials, the FSLN developed a disciplined program of political education using seminars for all popular organizations. The purpose of these seminars was not to inculcate a pre-conceived ideology into the participants, but rather to enable the people to reflect on their recent personal experiences in relation to the revolutionary changes underway. This approach developed class consciousness by helping people to think critically about their own history.

Family of a fallen "muchacho" beside the monument naming an avenue after their son.

Political education seminar held at the Central American University (UCA) in Managua.

Political education for workers began the last week of September and continued through early November, with a series of "Political and Trade Union Formation Seminars" sponsored by the CST.[6] At one CST meeting of about 75 union members in Masaya, Flor de María Monte Rey from the *Casa Sandinista* in Diriamba spoke to a full house about the dynamic relationship between the FSLN and the CST.[7] The workers wanted to know whether socialism would lead to suppression of political dissent. The answer came in practice as the formal talk was followed by a question-and-answer period in which some workers challenged the speaker. This kind of critical dialogue in turn strengthened the FSLN's unity with the workers and unions under the CST umbrella, since political dialogue was a rare thing under Somoza in any union.

"Political preparation" courses were held for students at all three levels—primary, secondary and university—in a week-long orientation before regular classes began. The goal of the orientation was to discuss the changes needed in the educational system so it could serve the revolutionary process. At a secondary school in Diriamba, for example, the course included speeches honoring student martyrs, political education about the FSLN, and a talk by the school's principal about the skills needed to build the revolution. Similarly, at the National Autonomous University (UNAN) the FSLN emphasized that instead of training lawyers, the faculty must prepare engineers and technicians who will make concrete contributions to the new society. The university also began creating student and professor brigades to work on the physical reconstruction of "the Nation of Sandino."[8] Perhaps the most impressive example of this new educational orientation is the 1980 literacy campaign which is sending thousands of students into the countryside. The purpose of this campaign is not only to educate illiterates but to deepen the class awareness of student-literacy teachers through living with the poor families they are teaching.

Christians, along with the rest of society, also needed to reassess their role in revolutionary Nicaragua. But unlike public or state organizations, the church had to voluntarily initiate its own political education. During the week of September 24-28, Christians attended a seminar entitled "Christian Faith and the Sandinista Revolution" at the Central American University (UCA) in Managua. Organized by Father Alvaro Argüello, a well-known Jesuit historian, the goal of the seminar was "to help Christians in Nicaragua understand how to make sense of their Christian faith and experience in the revolution."[9] The ecumenical seminar, slated as a Marxist-Christian dialogue, consisted of political presentations by representatives of the FSLN and theological reflections by Church leaders and teachers. Father Argüello outlined the task:

> If there is no theology to justify and orient the popular struggle against the dictatorship, a disjuncture will develop between the church and the popular masses... for it is through Christian participation at all levels that *the Sandinista revolution offers us—as Christians and as a Latin American Church—a new opportunity to show our authentic Christian character: firm solidarity, clear conscience and participation with all those who are committed to work for a profoundly human and national transformation.*[10]

The FSLN leaders participating in the seminar broke down stereotypes and reduced the fears which some Christians had about the ideological and political implications of the revolution for the church by reviewing the history of class struggle in Nicaragua. Through anecdotes about the suffering of the poor and affirmations of nationalism, the Sandinistas linked Christian ideas to the class struggle. One of the theologians who spoke at the seminar, Dr. Pablo Richard of Chile, elaborated on this theme when he reminded the audience that the Gospels are not opposed to the issue of class struggle, precisely because "love for the rich is different than love for the poor. To save both, the church must save the poor from their poverty and the rich from their riches."[11]

Musicians and poets abound in revolutionary Nicaragua.

Mass Media and the New Song Movement

*To create a nation is also to make a revolution....
Today, as owners of our history, we must recall all significant events of the past and link them with the present tasks of the revolution.*[12]

This statement by Julio López, FSLN Secretary of Propaganda and Education, reflects the goal of the new government to use the mass media for building political consciousness. It would do this by highlighting important historical events in the struggle against Somoza.

One such event occurred on September 21, the anniversary of the death of Anastasio Somoza García, the founder of the dynasty who was killed on that day in 1956 by the poet revolutionary Rigoberto López Pérez. Using the middle class media instrument, the new *Televisión Sandino*, an extensive history of the young patriot's life and sacrifice was splashed across Nicaragua's TV screens. The careful re-telling of that old history was necessary because the event had been so distorted by the dictatorship that most Nicaraguans knew little more than the fact that Rigoberto's heroic effort cost him his life. The TV presentation clarified the importance of his sacrifice: he broke the myth that no one could challenge the dynasty and in so doing, laid the groundwork for the formation of the FSLN.

The radio has been the most important medium of mass education in Nicaragua. In addition to regular news, the radio often broadcasts Ernesto Cardenal's prophetic interpretations of the Psalms. Cardenal, the Trappist prophet and pastor of Solentiname (a small group of islands in the southern portion of Lake Nicaragua) became Minister of Culture after the triumph. His popular gospel[13] and prophetic psalms, which first made Cardenal internationally famous, are now becoming a regular part of the new cultural-political education program. Another of Cardenal's important contributions has been the creation of the Teatro Popular Ruben Dario, a national center for popular theatre, dance and music.

However, music may be having an even more powerful impact on popular consciousness than the mass media. During the dictatorship, the so-called "new song movement"—resistance songs sung "underground"— helped build much broader opposition sentiment to Somoza than was politically evident. Clandestine song movement leader Carlos Mejía Godoy used to sing this conclusion to an indigenous Nicaraguan folk mass:

*There is nothing more beautiful than to look
at a people reunited
who fight when they seek to improve (things)
There is nothing more beautiful than to hear
in the song of everyone
a single, immense cry of fraternity.*[14]

Singing where and when they could during the reign of Somoza was a far cry, however, from the post-victory period when Mejía Godoy and musical groups like "Los de Palacaquina," "Pancasán," and others suddenly became part of every important public rally and political celebration. Nicaragua, the land of poets, is being educated politically today through the media of song. For instance, the Hymn of Sandinista Unity, which sums up the thrust of Nicaragua's new political education campaign, is heard everywhere:

*Let us march forward, companeros
let us advance to the Revolution
our people are owners of their history
architects of their liberation*

*Combatants of the Sandinista Front
forward, for that is our destiny
a black-and-red flag covers us
a free Country, Victory of Death!*

*Adelante marchemos compañeros
avancemos a la Revolucion
nuestro pueble es el dueno du su historia
arquitectos de su liberacion*

*Combatientes del Frente Sandinista
adelante que es nuestro porvenir
rojinegra bandera nos cobija
Patria libre, ¡Vencer o Morir!*[15]

92

MASS ORGANIZATIONS: YOUTH AND WOMEN

The Nicaraguan people had achieved a level of virtually complete popular participation in the struggle by the time of the final offensive—a critical factor in the successful overthrow of Somoza and in the subsequent struggle to build a new participatory society. Mass organizations provided the context for the people to continue their high level of involvement in bringing about the revolution's social, economic, and political goals. Along with the CDS, ATC, and CST, which were all created in the workplace or neighborhood, two mass organizations were formed which spoke to the needs of specific sectors of society: youth and women.

Juventud Sandinista

"The vanguard and Nicaragua's youth have *always* been united," emphasized Carlos Carrion on September 15, during an event officially constituting the "Sandinista Youth, 19th of July."[1] But the post-victory period required the development of a new relationship between the FSLN as vanguard and the thousands of its young combatants.[2] The

Nicaragua's next generation of Sandinistas.

Uniformed students form a procession waiting for their turn to march in

FSLN needed to continue to develop the political and social awareness which Somoza's corruption had awakened in so many "children of Sandino," but these young people could not continue in their role of combatants. They needed to return to school and to their families, and participate in the revolutionary process from those places in society.

There was also a need to consolidate the many student and youth organizations which had sprung up against the dictatorship, particularly those student groups directly linked to the FSLN. Sandinista Youth, July 19th, *Juventud Sandinista* (JS), became that synthesizing revolutionary youth organization. The largest groups incorporated into JS were the Revolutionary Nicaraguan Youth (JRN), the Revolutionary Sandinista Youth (JRS), and the Federation of Revolutionary Students (FER).[3] Initially the JS's particular task was to unite the youth who had joined the FSLN as combatants or militia, but quickly it encompassed a much broader representation of Nicaraguan young people.

JS organized on a national level with local chapters across the country, and soon initiated fraternal relations with international youth organizations. Chapters organized young people not only in schools, but in work places—fac-

Sandino Stadium on September 19.

tories and plantations—to ensure a relationship with all sectors of society.[4]

Local JS groups gathered for historical and political reflection to help understand the changes taking place and to take an active part in that process. On September 19, for example, JS issued a condemnation of political opportunists who were subverting the revolution through self-interested actions.[5] The development of this criticism was just as important an exercise in political education within JS as it was a public statement.

Juventud Sandinista also used special brigades to develop political and social awareness in the young people. During September these brigades went to the poorest *barrios* to assist with food distribution and neighborhood clean-up. These activities helped bring together middle and upper class young with the working class.[6]

As Nicaragua prepared to begin classes at the end of September—classes which the final offensive had interrupted—JS played a crucial role, organizing within the student population and encouraging young people to return to their studies even though so much exciting activity was going on outside the classroom.

On September 19, the traditional Nicaraguan independence day, students representing public and private schools from all across the capital city gathered at the newly renamed Sandino Stadium. More than 40,000 uniformed students marched with their classmates, banners held high and music playing loudly. One observer commented that never in the history of Somoza had students held such a large celebration that was "all their own."[7]

FLSN commander Luis Carrion addressed the excited crowd of young people:

Gathered here today are representatives of our students and youth—the generation which will shortly move into life with immense responsibilities for the revolutionary process. Young people, you showed an immense heroism and self sacrifice in the struggle against the dictatorship. Today you must apply that same spirit to study and discipline....In the last few years of the dictatorship it was impossible to be a student; no conscientious student could calmly sit in classrooms while the armed hordes of somocistas *assassinated friends in the streets outside. You had to be a patriot first, then a student. For that you were expelled and hunted by (Somoza's) Office of Security.*[8]

Carrion went on to say that the old society had always converted students into an intellectual elite above the masses and above manual labor. This would be no more.

You shall intimately embrace the working class. From them you will learn discipline, humbleness; to them you must go as humble teachers of the alphabet, humble helpers in the work of the countryside maintaining a tight and indestructible unity between the students, teachers and all the people of Nicaragua. This is what it means to build the homeland, to build the revolution.[9]

Associacion de Mujeres Nicaraguenses "Luisa Amanda Espinosa"

The Association of Nicaraguan Women Confronting the National Problem (AMPRONAC) faced the same post-victory reality that all the resistance groups faced. With the successful toppling of the dictatorship, the organization's tasks in one sense, were over. This did not mean that AMPRONAC no longer served a purpose; rather, that women's organizations needed to change in order to respond to the tasks of the new era.[10] AMPRONAC chapters across the country reflected on this and sought the correct change. The Rivas chapter, for example, announced on August 31 that it had changed its name to the Federation of Sandinista Women, using the slogan, "For the Rights of the Woman, Sandinista Women Stand Ready."[11]

Women realized that they had played a critical role in the anti-dictatorial struggle, but that their work had not ended. The experience of men and women fighting side by side had significantly advanced the process of liberating women, but it could not change the social patterns overnight. Generations of dependency and oppression not only from men, but also from the Somocist and imperialist structures of domination themselves meant the hardest struggles were

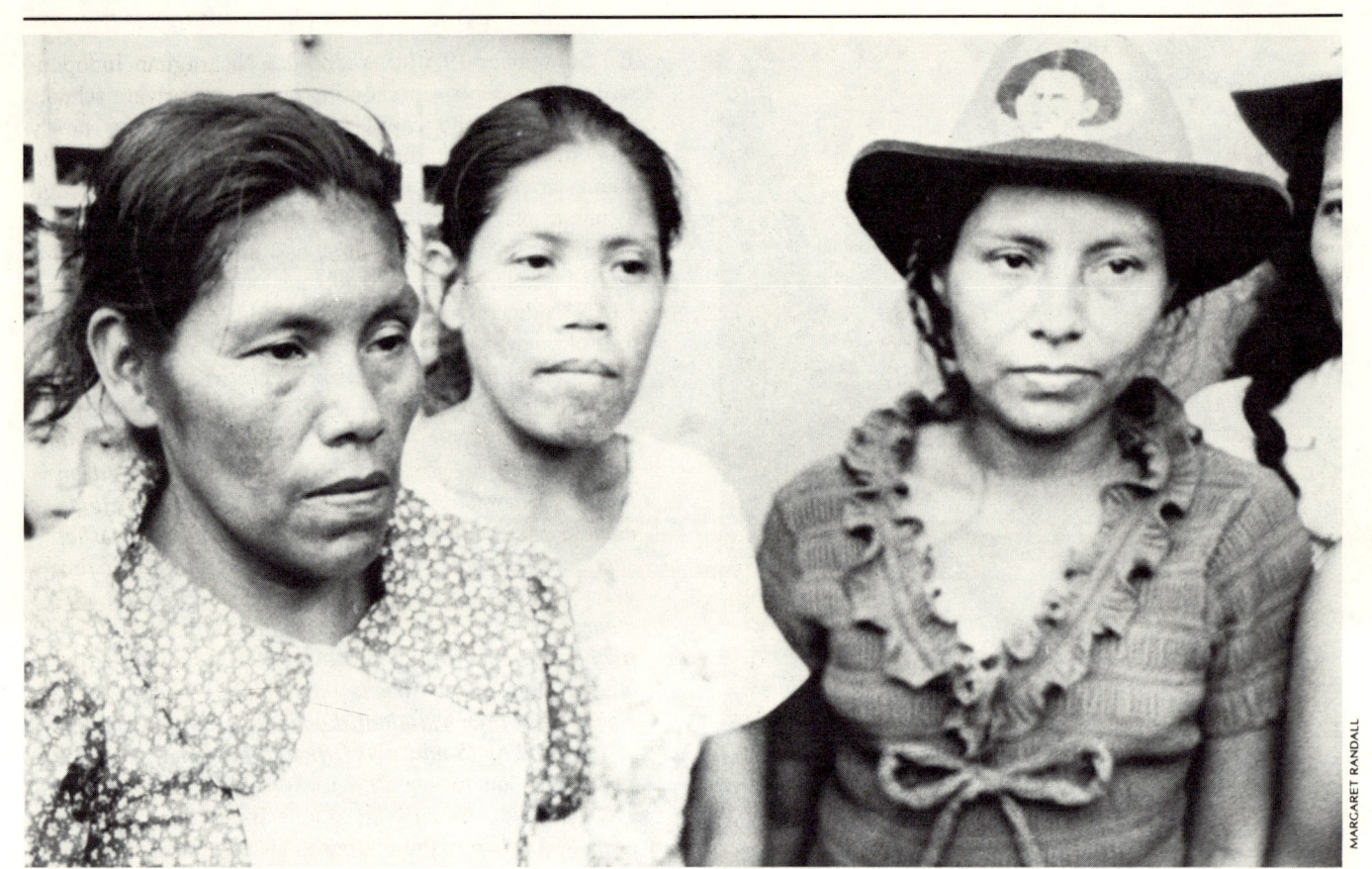

Peasant women of Cua are clear in their determination to be integral participants in Nicaraguan Women's Association. Woman on far right: Angela Diaz Aguilar.

still before them. However, women realized that their personal struggle had to be integrated with the goal of rebuilding the new society. Only through their efforts would revolutionary Nicaragua effect full equality between women and men.

The name AMPRONAC no longer corresponded to the tasks of the new era. The organization now became the Association of Nicaraguan Women, adding the sub-title: Luisa Amanda Espinosa. Luisa Amanda, a young peasant killed in 1970, was the first woman in the FSLN to fall in combat. Her life represented a level of commitment which all Nicaraguan women could aspire to achieve.[12]

The Association made a particular commitment to incorporate *campesina* women. They formed groups in the rural Pacific coastal area during September-November. On December 16, 1979, 700 women from rural communities held the first "Assembly of Campesina Women," providing a national forum for women to reflect on their traditional role in society and seek common solutions to problems.[13] The women at the conference raised as a priority the issue of child care on the state farms. The Women's Assocation began to work with the Ministry of Agricultural Development (MIDA) to address this and other needs of *campesina* women.[14]

Other activities of the Association included the development of women's brigades which joined the CDS and other clean-up and reconstruction brigades; health brigades which worked with the Ministry of Health; plans for constructing public laundry centers, cafeterias, and infant care centers; and fundraising events to assist in work with women on the Atlantic coast.

The Association of Nicaraguan Women recognized that education implies empowerment and that the process of becoming literate is of utmost importance to the integration of women in to the country's revolutionary process. They therefore concentrated their energies during the fall on preparation for the 1980 literacy crusade. The Association assisted with the nationwide census to determine accurate social statistics. It was not surprising that the statistics revealed an illiteracy rate much higher among women than that of the overall national illiteracy rate of 53%.

Through the Association of Nicaraguan Women, the Nicaraguan liberating process was also shared with women in other Central and South American countries. Domitilla Barrios de Chugora, a Bolivian woman known for her organizing of housewives in the mining camps of Bolivia, came to Nicaragua in November and shared the experiences of Bolivian women with her Nicaraguan counterparts.[15]

Another foreign visitor was Margaret Randall, American feminist and writer living in Cuba. Famous for her writings about Latin American women, Randall is particularly known for her biography of the life of Doris Tijerino.[16] She spoke eloquently to Nicaraguan women, saying she believed that women's participation in the Nicaraguan struggle was equalled only by that of Vietnamese women. Margaret expressed the reality which women from an oppressed society could understand well:

Women (especially from the third world and Latin

America) seek their liberation within the liberation struggle of their whole people. The two cannot be separated.[17]

Through the Nicaraguan Women's Association, women are developing a fuller consciousness of the role they must take within Nicaragua's revolutionary process. A *Barricada* editorial expressed the challenge of the future:

With the triumph of the revolution we must begin our fight against economic dependency, misery, ignorance...and women must assume their share of the tasks in the organized, disciplined, consistent manner they held against the dictatorhsip....In the society we are constructing...discriminatory relationships have no place. A Woman has the right to be considered a full human being, full Nicaraguan. She has the right to... education, health care, work,...and to enjoy the fruits of her labor. But it is fundamentally the women themselves who must carry this struggle forward....They are the ones who must through organizing themselves, conquer their rightful place in the building of a society of free women and men. This struggle must be supported by all companeros, so that all emerge victorious against ideological backwardness.[18]

The Dawn which yesterday was a temptation, today is a reality. Free Nicaragua!

NEW FOREIGN POLICY: NON-ALIGNMENT

Symbolic of its new foreign policy direction, Nicaragua joined the Non-Aligned bloc at its Sixth Summit meeting in Havana, Cuba in early September 1979. Cuba, which for years was the hemisphere's only representative, this year became the Triennial President of the 94-nation body. Along with Nicaragua, the addition of Grenada and Surinam (plus Argentina, Cuba, Guyana, Jamaica, Panama, Peru and Trinidad and Tobago, who were previous representatives) consolidated the "Latin American participation in this Movement,"[1] making its representation now more than 10% of the total.[2]

FSLN Commander Daniel Ortega was welcomed at the plenary session of the Sixth Summit with a tremendous, standing ovation. The Sandinista leader, dressed in military fatigues—symbolic of the struggle that had been raging only six weeks earlier—asked for the effective solidarity of the Non-Aligned nations in order to help Nicaragua overcome the "terrible economic and financial crisis which dominates our Central American country as a consequence of the pillage and tyranny of Somoza."[3] The young commander did not limit his definition of the threat to Nicaragua in monetary terms alone:

We know that imperialism is interested in making our process fail and that it is going to utilize all the resources within its grasp to fulfill that goal. Today, more than ever, we need the disinterested support of the Non-Aligned nations and we believe that the consolidation of our revolution is a challenge to this Movement.[4]

Ortega denounced the reactionary sectors in the United States as particularly responsible for this campaign against Nicaragua, and he condemned the U.S. blockade of Cuba and its continued occupation of Guantanamo Bay. He also expressed solidarity with the people of Vietnam, the Popular Government of Cambodia, the struggle in Zimbabwe, the Grenadian revolution and support for the independence of Puerto Rico. He concluded his address to the enthusiastic Third World body: "As we are generous in victory; so shall we be inflexible in our defense of the revolution."[5]

International Solidarity Visits

During the first months of the revolution various Central American government leaders plus the Prime Minister of Vietnam visited Nicaragua to express their pro-Sandinista solidarity. Two examples stand out. On August 18, General Omar Torrijos, Commander of the Panamanian National Guard, was received by a huge crowd. It included not only Nicaraguan authorities but also a contingent of children and the Mayor of Monimbo, all of whom had physically fought against the dictatorship. Torrijos was particularly remembered as the one who wept upon hearing of the death of Commander German Pomares. During the massive recep-

96

tion for him in the Plaza of the Revolution, Torrijos said, "Upon each square meter of this plaza stands the highest percentage of popular dignity that can be found in the Americas." [6]

At a deeper level of revolutionary solidarity, Phan Van Dong, representing the Socialist Republic of Vietnam, arrived in Nicaragua from the Non-Aligned meeting and said, "Like the Vietnamese people, you have made enormous sacrifices in your struggle-to-the-death against ferocious and perfidious enemies....this represents the victory of a people who with determination rose up to fight the oppressive yoke of imperialism." [7] The great empathy felt by these two societies for each other was reflected in the welcoming message by Commander Carlos Nunez:

Revolutionary solidarity is international: the peoples of every society are brothers and sisters, and it is the people who break down the barriers. We say very frankly that just as the counter-revolutionary forces could not defeat Vietnam, neither will they be able to defeat Nicaragua. [8]

Changing Regional Dynamics: Popular Solidarity

The immediate result of these changing international relationships inspired by the Sandinista victory is a dramatic shift in the political dynamics of the region. The equilibrium has shifted away from imperialism and the various ruling elites. The decisive weight in this shifting balance is the role of the people and their mass organizations both in response to the Sandinista cause and in terms of the growing unity within their own national struggles.

One example of this solidarity with the Sandinista cause was made explicit on the occasion of the transfer of former U.S.-Zonian-held property back to the Republic of Panama on October 1, 1979. During the main event of that decolonization celebration—attended by 400,000 persons—when the Nicaraguan delegation was introduced, even though it was not allowed to speak, the multitudes broke into vociferous cheering and applause that lasted more than 15 minutes. This expression of popular support for the Nicaraguan victory was something the officials at the podium could not control. [9] While popular opinion and governmental policy often do not coincide, certainly throughout Central America today, all governments are now taking this pro-Sandino spirit seriously.

Equally important, lessons from the Nicaraguan struggle are already being reflected in other regional conflicts. Two examples stand out. First, the importance of unifying left vanguard elements. In January, 1980, the four principal popular vanguard organizations in El Salvador formed a strategic alliance called the *Coordinadora Nacional* which serves as the principal progressive leadership in the country. [10] Second, the merging of progressive popular groups into a united front. Thus in Guatemala some 150 organizations representing most of the social and labor groups in the country created the Democratic Front Against Repression (FDCR), the main opposition to General Lucas' military regime. [11] While each of these countries has its own long history of struggle, distinct reality, and unique form of organizing, the Nicaraguan revolution has clearly impacted and speeded up these neighboring processes of radical change.

Reaction to These Dynamics: Repression and Isolation

These changing popular dynamics have produced a political reassessment of traditional strategies by U.S. imperialism and the dictatorships in the region. As of April 1980, there were at least four elements making up the new strategy aimed at containing the Nicaraguan revolution: hard-line militarism, moderation-through-reform, isolation, and regional restructuring of alliances.

First, the hard-line militarism tactic refers primarily to the military governments of Guatemala and El Salvador, and to a lesser degree, Honduras. The Pentagon and CIA have argued consistently since July 19, 1979 that the United States must continue to supply weapons to the rightist military regimes in Central America in order to avoid the "Nicaraguanization of the region." [12] Various reports have indicated that Guatemala has amassed forces on its border with El Salvador and is willing to send in troops if requested by the Salvadorean military. Apparently, Guatemala wants to make El Salvador a "buffer zone" against the spread of revolutionary ferment across its border which might join the significant left forces within its own country. At the same time, the Carter administration has sent military advisors

The FSLN high command continues today to hold strong its commitment

and "up to $7 million in military sales and credits to El Salvador in an effort to prop up its faltering new government and block a leftist takeover."[13]

Second, the moderation-through-reform tactic is clearly the one being applied to El Salvador by the United States. Shortly after the Nicaraguan victory in August 1979, high U.S. State Department official Viron Vakey visited El Salvador and expressed his grave concerns about the radicalizing dynamics there. Then, on October 15, 1979 a *coup d'etat* against the repressive regime of Carlos Humberto Romero was carried out by some "moderate" colonels in the Salvadorean army which received immediate and unconditional approval from Washington. The new military promised a series of reforms—including the nationalization of banks and the redistribution of land, which the United States agreed to fund but which are opposed by the oligarchy.[14] Even though all the liberal-to-progressive groups invited to join the new experiment by the military had resigned by December 1979 (except the Christian Democrats), the mounting repression is far more real than the promised reforms (600 political assassinations in the first two months of 1980).[15] Meanwhile, the State Department continues to justify this "soft stick" approach in its anxious effort to mollify rising popular demands sufficiently to prevent "another Nicaragua."[16]

The third tactic is that of isolating Nicaragua. No overt political or economic measures to isolate Nicaragua have occurred as yet—although there is significant resistance in Congress to grant aid to the Government of National Reconstruction. But the history of the U.S. embargo of Cuba over the years, and the heightened aggressiveness towards the Cuban revolution by the Carter administration in the early fall of 1979, suggests that this could happen to Nicaragua as events in the region exacerbate. The strategy to isolate Nicaragua may, however, focus less on anti-FSLN aggressiveness and more on containment, i.e., preventing the spread of the Nicaraguan revolution to other countries in the region. On the other hand, while the FSLN is clear that it must first consolidate its own revolution, it has no intention of restricting itself in terms of developing any and all relationships it deems legitimate, such as its ties with the government of Grenada. Leaders of that revolution recently visited Nicaragua where they received a warm welcome.[17]

Finally, in terms of the tactic of restructuring regional alliances, the future of CONDECA comes into question now that its traditional center, Somoza's National Guard, has been dispersed. The reactionary military and para-military forces of that old alliance are even now involved in mobilizations aimed at destroying the left in El Salvador. Among these recent moves are: the reunification of former National Guardsmen who had fled to Honduras, El Salvador and Guatemala (some 7-8,000) and are now being consolidated into the Salvadorean army or are operating as mercenaries; the transporting of Guatemalan mercenaries into El Savador coordinated by retired general, Carlos Alberto Medrano, the founder of ORDEN,[18] and Guatemala's ex-Vice President Salvador Alarcon;[19] meetings in Miami between Cuban exiles, Somoza aides, and Guatemala officials; and

to the Nicaraguan people and carry forward the principles of the revolution.

reports of the recruiting of Cuban mercenaries in Miami and New Orleans. All of these moves seem to point to the fact that Guatemala has become the new northern pole of the regional CONDECA forces while the southern pole continues to be the U.S. military bases in Panama.

Conclusion

One thing is clear: the Sandinista victory has set off a chain reaction. In toppling Somoza, the FSLN disturbed the delicate balance of dependency relationships and domination which imperialism had set up in the hemisphere. This happened at the very moment when the social conditions of suffering and unemployment are so extreme, that the Latin American people have few alternatives and are prepared to sacrifice everything to bring about a significant change. The Sandinista victory has given the whole region a heightened sense of its popular autochthonous unity, and hope has been engendered among the masses.[20]

This new spirit marks the begining of the end of that long history of artificially-created competition and conflict between the peoples of Central America.[21] The intra-nation tensions and regional hostilities are clearly by-products of structures of dependency between national elites and U.S. imperialism that date back to 1898. Thus it is not surprising that the Nicaraguan people in triumphing over *somocismo* have inevitably taken on an increased sense of their regional commitment. They now frequently refer to themselves as *centroamericanistas*. Prophetically, Sandino wrote long ago:[22]

"The present lies with the peoples of Hispanic America to whom I speak. When a government does not represent the aspirations of its citizens, these people - who gave that government its power - have the right to be represented by virile men and women and by ideas of an effective democracy, and not be useless puppets without moral value or patriotism who shame the pride of our race.

We are ninety million Hispanic Americans and we only need reflect on our unification to understand that Yankee imperialism is the most brutal enemy that threatens us and the only one which is determined to end through conquest our racial honor and the freedom of our peoples.

Tyrants do not represent nations, and liberty is not won with flowers."

Augusto Cesar Sandino

FOOTNOTES

The Somoza Legacy: Economic Bankruptcy

1. Center for International Policy, statistics compiled from U.S. AID, I.D.B., and U.N. ECLA, Washington, September, 1979.
2. *Wall Street Journal,* New York, July 18, 1979.
3. *Excelsior,* "Si occidente no ayuda irémos donde sea," Mexico, August 14, 1979, p. 2.
4. United Nations Economic and Social Council, Economic Committee on Latin America (CEPAL), "Nicaragua: Economic Repercussions of Recent Political Events," September, 1978, p. 17.
5. CEPAL, p. 36.
6. Jarquin, Edmundo, "The Nicaraguan Crisis and the International Monetary Fund," Washington, D.C., mimeographed document, May 10, 1979.
7. CEPAL, p. 42.
8. CEPAL, p. 25.
9. CEPAL, p. 20.
10. CEPAL, pp. 21-23.
11. CEPAL, p. 34.
12. *Wall Street Journal,* July 18, 1979.
13. *Washington Post,* July 26, 1979.
14. Telegram to the National Network in Solidarity with Nicaragua (and to others), from Michael Blumenthal, May 1979.
15. EPICA interview, Central Bank staff, Managua, September 1979.
16. Statement of Daniel Ortega before the U.N. General Assembly, September 28, 1979, (mimeographed translation).
17. *Washington Post,* July 26, 1979.
18. *Washington Post,* July 23, 1979.
19. *New York Times,* October 11, 1979.
20. *Latin American Weekly Report* (79, 08) December 21, 1979. also *Barricada,* November 14, 1979.

Sandinista Defense Committees: Popular Political Base

1. EPICA interview, the FSLN's regional CDS coordinator, Managua, September 1979.
2. Leo Gabriel, "Sin Discursos ni Consignas Rombantes, Se Izo la Bandera Roji-Negra," *Informativo Ciila-Cencos,* Mexico, July 24, 1979.
3. as heard on *Radio Sandino,* Managua, September 1979
4. *LAPR,* Vol. XIII, No. 42, October 26, 1979, London.
5. *Juventud Rebelde,* Havana, Cuba, July 28, 1979.
6. FSLN, *Los CDS!* Oficina de Propaganda del FSLN, September 1979, (pamphlet).
7. *Barricada,* July 25, 1979, p.3.
8. *Barricada,* July 25, 1979, p.3.
9. Epica interview in Rivas, September, 1979
10. *La Prensa,* August 20, 1979.

Agrarian Reform: Foundation of the Revolution

1. *El Programa de Gobierno y Nuestra Reforma Agraria,* Managua, 1979, INRA publication.
2. *Barricada,* September 21, 1979.
3. *Barricada,* December 22, 1979.
4. "Conference on Agrarian Reform," Nicaragua, February 11-14, 1980, co-sponsored by the INRA and the Land Tenure Center, Univ. of Wisconsin.
5. *Objetivos y Alcance de la Reforma Agraria Nicaraguense,* Managua, 1979, INRA publication.
6. *Barricada,* October 19, 1979.
7. Tirado, Manlio, "Hacen comunas en tierras de Somoza," *Excelsior,* September 19, 1979.
8. *Barricada,* September 21, 1979.
9. Tirado, Manlio.
10. *Barricada,* November 6, 1979.
11. *Latin American Weekly Report* (79-08), London, December 21, 1979.
12. *Latin American Commodities Report,* London, Vol.III, No.32, August 17, 1979.
13. *Barricada,* December 22, 1979.
14. EPICA interview, Managua, September 1979.

Labor Organizing: The ATC and CST

1. *Barricada,* July 26, 1979, p.i.
2. *Barricada,* July 26, 1979, p.4.
3. *Barricada,* October 12, 1979, p.10.
4. *Barricada,* August 12, 1979, p.4.
5. EPICA interview, INRA representatives, Chinandega, September 1979.
6. EPICA interview, banana workers, Standard Fruit packing plant, El Viejo, September 1979.
7. EPICA interview, CST representatives, Masaya, September 1979.
8. Roberto Lopez, International Representative of the UAW, General Motors Department, "Nicaraguan Trip," November 30, 1979.
9. William Dougherty, AIFLD Director, remarks, "Miami Conference on the Caribbean," *EPICA Report,* Washington, D.C., December 1979.
10. *La Prensa,* September 19, 1979, p. 9.
11. *Barricada,* September 25, 1979, pp. 1 and 10.

Rising Social and Political Problems

1. *La Prensa,* September 19, 1979, p.10.
2. *Barricada,* September 24, 1979, pp.1, 10.
3. *Barricada,* September 26, 1979, p.10.
4. Signs seen in Managua, September 1979.
5. *La Prensa,* September 19, 1979, p.10.
6. *La Prensa,* September 19, 1979, p.9.
7. *Barricada,* September 11, 1979, p.9.
8. *Barricada,* August 12, 1979, p.1.
9. *Barricada,* July 30, 1979, p.3.
10. *Barricada,* August 9, 1979, p.1.

Popular Political Education

1. *Barricada,* August 1, 1979, p.3.
2. *Barricada,* August 1, 1979, p.4.
3. *Barricada,* August 1, 1979, p.3.
4. *Barricada,* August 16, 1979, p.6.
5. *Barricada,* August 16, 1979, p.1.
6. *Barricada,* September 25, 1979, p.1.
7. EPICA interview, CST members, Masaya, September 1979.
8. *Barricada,* September 19, 1979, p.9.
10. *La Prensa,* September 23, 1979, p.9.
11. *La Prensa,* September 28, 1979, p.9.
12. Ernesto Cardenal, *The Gospel in Solentiname,* Orbis Books: New York, 1976.
13. *Barricada,* September 11, 1979, pp.1, 12.
14. El Taller de Sonido Popular, "Canto de Despedida," *Misa Campesina Nicaraguense*
15. Carlos Mejia Godoy, *Himno de la Unidad Sandinista.*

Mass Organizations: Youth and Women

1. *Barricada,* September 15, 1979.
2. *Barricada,* August 3, 1979.
3. *Barricada,* December 31, 1979.
4. EPICA interview, Managua headquarters of *Juventud Sandinista,* September 1979.
5. *Barricada,* September 19, 1979.
6. EPICA interview with *Juventud Sandinista* brigadistas, September 1979.
7. EPICA interview, Sandino Stadium, Managua, September 1979.
8. *Barricada,* September 16, 1979.
9. *Barricada,* September 16, 1979.
10. *Barricada,* August 9, 1979.
11. *Barricada,* August 31, 1979.
12. AMNLAE, documents from the *Casa de las Mujeres,* Managua, September 1979. (mimeographed, no title).
13. *Barricada,* December 31, 1979.
14. *Barricada,* December 31, 1979.
15. *Barricada,* November 13, 1979.
16. Margaret Randall, *Doris Tijerino: Inside the Nicaraguan Revolution,* New Star Books, Ltd: Vancouver, 1978.
17. *Barricada,* November 13, 1979.
18. *Barricada,* November 16, 1979.

New Foreign Policy: Non-Alignment

1. *Barricada,* September 5, 1979, p. 2.
2. Hemispheric observers included: Barbados, Bolivia, Brazil, Colombia, Costa Rica, Dominica, Ecuador, El Salvador, Mexico, Santa Lucia, Uruguay, Venezuela and the Puerto Rican Socialist Party (PSP).
3. *Barricada,* September 7, 1979, p. 8.
4. *Barricada,* September 7, 1979, p. 1.
5. *Barricada,* September 7, 1979, p. 1.
6. *Barricada,* August 19, 1979, p. 1.
7. *Barricada,* September 15, 1979, p. 3.
8. *Barricada,* September 14, 1979, p. 12.
9. EPICA staff report, Panama City, October 1, 1979.
10. The *Coordinadora Nacional* is made up of the Popular Revolutionary Bloc (BPR), Front for United Political Action (FAPU), Popular Leagues (LP-28), and the National Democratic Union (UDN).
11. Document of the *"Frente Democrático Contra la Represión,"* Guatemala, Fall 1979.
12. *Le Monde Diplomatique,* "El Salvador: El Eslabón Más Pequeño," September 1979.
13. *Washington Post,* February 14, 1980.
14. Barbara Koeppel, "Face-Off in San Salvador", *The Nation,* March 8, 1980, p. 276.
15. Roman Catholic Legal Office, San Salvador, March, 1980.
16. Cynthia Arnson, "Washington Talks Intervention," *The Nation,* March 8, 1980, p. 274.
17. *Barricada,* 1980, p. 1.
18. WOLA, "El Salvador: Human Rights and U.S. Economic Policy," Wash., D.C., Jan. 1979, p. 9.
19. *Central America Update,* LAWG, Toronto, February, 1980.
20. For example, the historic unity between Farabundo Martí of El Salvador and Augusto César Sandino in Las Segovias, Nicaragua.
21. For example, the artificially-created "Soccer War" between Honduras and El Salvador in 1979.
22. Sandino, "Letter to the Governors of (Hispanic) America", El Chipotón, Las Segovias, Nicaragua, August 4, 1928.

SELECTED BIBLIOGRAPHY

Nicaragua: Reforma o Revolucion. 3 vols. Managua: n.p. 1978.

Coyuntura Economica y Politica. Managua: n.p. 1979.

Pensamiento Critico: La Lucha de Clases en Nicaragua. 3 vols. Managua: n.p. 1979.

Barreto, Pablo Emilio. *44 Anos de Dictadura Somocista.* Managua: *La Prensa,* 1978.

Cardenal, Ernesto. *The Gospel in Solentiname.* 2 vols. Maryknoll, N.Y.: Orbis Books, 1976.

Chamorro, Pedro Joaquin. *Estirpe Sangrienta: Los Somozas.* 4th ed., Managua: Ediciones El Pez y La Serpiente, 1978.

Comando, Juan Jose Quezada. *Frente Sandinista: Diciembre Victorioso.* Mexico City: Editorial Diogenes, 1976.

Comite Cristiano de Solidaridad con el Pueblo de Nicaragua (CRISOL). *Monimbo: Trajedia y Simbolo de Liberacion.* Managua, 1979.

Desme, Carlos Sobenes. *Asalto al Palacio Nacional de Nicaragua.* Managua: n.p. 1979.

El Pensamiento Vivo de Sandino. 5th ed. San Jose, Costa Rica: Editorial Universitaria Centroamericana (EDUCA), 1979.

Millet, Richard. *Guardians of the Dynasty.* Maryknoll, N.Y.: Orbis Books, 1979.

Quijano, Carlos. *Nicaragua: Un Pueblo, Una Revolucion.* Mexico City: Editorial Pueblo Nuevo, 1978.

Ryan, John Morris, et al. *Area Handbook on Nicaragua.* Washington, D.C.: U.S. Government Printing Office, 1970.

Sanchez, Mayo Antonio. *Nicaragua: Ano Cero.* Mexico City: Editorial Diana, 1979.

Encuentro: La Realidad Nacional. Managua: Universidad Centroamericana, 1978.

Wheelock, Jaime. *Imperialismo y Dictadura.* 2nd ed. Mexico City: Editores Siglo Veintiuno, 1978.

REPORTS, DOCUMENTS, PERIODICALS AND ARTICLES

AMPRONAC, Documentos de Ampronac. Managua: AMNLAE, 1978 (pamphlet).

Arnson, Cynthia. "Washington Talks Intervention." *The Nation.* 8 March 1980.

Barricada. Managua, July 1979-February 1980.

Bendana, Alejandro. "Crisis in Nicaragua." *NACLA Report on the Americas.* November-December 1979.

CENCOS. *Informativo Cencos-Ciila.* Mexico City, 1978-1979 (reports).

Center for International Policy FACT SHEET. *The Impact of War in Nicaragua.* Washington, D.C. 1979 (statistics).

Comite Mexicano en Solidaridad con el Pueblo de Nicaragua. *Sandino y la Libercion.* Mexico City, issues 1976-1979.

"Dios Une a Sandinoamerica." *Dialogo,* Guatemala City, August-September 1979.

Frente Democratico Contra la Represion. *Documento del FDCR.* Guatemala, fall 1979 (mimeographed document).

Harnecker, Marta. "La Estrategia del la Victoria." *Bohemia.* Havana, December 1979, pp. 2-17 (an interview with Commander Humberto Ortega).

Jarquin, Edmundo. *The Nicaraguan Crisis and the International Monetary Fund.* Washington, D.C., 10 May 1979. (mimeographed unpublished document)

Koeppel, Barbara. "Face Off in El Salvador." *The Nation,* 8 March 1980.

La Prensa. Managua, fall 1977-February 1980.

Latin American Political Reports. London, 1978, 1979, 1980.

Lopez, Robert. *Nicaragua Trip.* Detroit, 30 November 1979. (report to the United Auto Workers, General Motors Division).

Marques, Gabriel Garcia. "Casa de los Chanchos." *Sandino Vive, Nicaragua Vencera.* Panama, September 1979.

New York Committee on Nicaragua. *Nicaragua: Emergency in the Land of Volcanoes.* New York, fall 1978 (pamphlet).

"Nicaragua." *NACLA North American and Empire Report.* February 1976.

Nicaragua: Dictatorship and Revolution. London: Latin American Bureau, 1979 (special brief).

Nicaragua: Song and Struggle. Minneapolis: Nicaraguan Solidarity Committee of Minnesota, Summer 1979 (pamphlet).

"Nicaragua: Troubled Economy." *Central America Report.* no 42. California, October 1978.

Nicaragua Update (through September 1978) and *Central America Update* 1979-1980. Vancouver, British Columbia: Community Information Resource Group (newsletter).

Permanent Commission on Human Rights. *Formas y Alcances de la Violacion a los Derechos Humanos en Nicaragua.* Managua, March 1979 (and other documents throughout 1978-1979).

Rodriquez, Arsenio, "Nicaragua: Principio del Fin de Una Dinastia?" *Tricontinental Especial,* Havana, 1979, pp. 4-13.

Victor Sanabria Documentation Center. San Jose, Costa Rica, 1978 and 1979 (newsletters on human rights violations in Nicaragua).

United Nations Economic and Social Council. *Nicaragua: Economic Repercussions of Recent Political Events.* New York, 1979 (report of the Economic Committee on Latin America

United Nations High Commission on Refugees. *Report on the Refugee Situation in Latin America.* New York, 1978-1979.

Waksman Schinca, Daniel. "Interview with Tomas Borge. "*El Dia,* Mexico City, 19 April 1979.

Walker, Thomas. *An Evaluation of the Carter Administration's Human Rights Policy in Nicaragua.* Ohio University, fall 1979 (unpublished report).

Wheelock, Jaime. "Entrevista." *Causa Sandinista.* no 5. San Jose, Costa Rica, November 1978, pp. 1-16.

Washington Office on Latin America. "El Salvador: Human Rights and U.S. Economic Policy." *Latin American Update.* January 1979.

DECLARATIONS, COMMUNIQUES AND FLYERS

ATC. "La ATC: Organizacion Sandinista de los Trabajadores del Campo." Managua, Coleccion Oscar Robelo, September 1979 (mimeographed reports).

ATC. *El Machete.* Nicaragua, 1978 (occasional, illegal newsletter).

FAO. "Declaracion del Frente Amplio de Oposicion." Nicaragua, 5 October 1978 (flyer).

FAO. "Programa Democratico del Gobierno Nacional del FAO." Nicaragua, October 1978 (flyer)

FSLN. "Atencion!!! Pueblo de Nicaragua." Nicaragua, September 1978 (mimeographed publication of the Tendencia Proletaria).

FSLN. FSLN Foreign Affairs Commission. *Lucha Sandinista.* Nicaragua, 3 June 1978.

FSLN. Secretaria Nacional de Propaganda y Educacion, "Los CDS." September 1979.

FSLN. *Unidad Sandinista* Panama City, 1979 (official FSLN

publication following unification).

Inter-American Commission on Human Rights in Central America. "Special Bulletin on the Judgment of Somoza as a War Criminal." San Jose, Costa Rica, 15 November 1978.

INRA. "El Programa de Gobierno y Nuestra Reforma Agraria." Managua, fall 1979 (government pamphlet).

INRA. "Objectivos y Alcances de la Reforma Agraria Nicaraguense." Managua, fall 1979 (government pamphlet).

Juventud Nicaraguense Revolucionario. "Participacion de la Juventud en la Lucha Popular Contra la Dictadura Somocista." Managua, November 1979 (mimeographed document).

Much of the information which documents the last two years of the Sandinista struggle was produced clandestinely in Nicaragua or other Central American countries. Little publishing information is available for such books, periodicals and flyers. We have attempted to supply descriptive information where hard data is lacking.

GLOSSARY

AMPRONAC—Association of Nicaraguan Women Confronting the National Problem (pre-victory).

AMNLAE—Association of Nicaraguan Women "Luisa Amanda Espinoza" (post-victory).

ATC—Association of Rural Workers

BECAT—Special Brigades Against Terrorist Acts; special forces of the National Guard.

CDC—Civilian Defense Committee (block organizations of the FSLN and MPU (pre-victory).

CDS—Sandinista Defense Committee (replacing the CDC after victory.

CEPA—Agricultural Promotion Education Center (church-related).

CONDECA—Council for Central American Defense (a creation of the Inter-American Defense Board, Washington, D.C.).

CPDH—Permanent Commission on Human Rights, Nicaragua.

CONFER—National Conference of Nicaraguan Religious Organizations.

COSEP—Superior Council of Private Enterprise.

FAO—Broad Opposition Front (upper-class political coalition which opposed Somoza but sought a modified status-quo).

FSLN—Sandinista Front for National Liberation.

GPP—Prolonged Popular War tendency of the FSLN.

IMF—International Monetary Fund.

INDE—Institute for Nicaraguan Development (conservative business organization).

INRA—National Institute of Agrarian Reform (post-victory).

JS—Sandinista Youth, 19th of July (post-victory).

MIDA—Ministry of Agricultural Development (post-victory).

MILPAS—Popular *campesino* Militia which resisted Somoza.

MPU—United People's Movement (a broad-based popular front organization of the FSLN).

OAS—Organization of American States.

PLI—Independent Liberal Party (split from the Liberal Party when Somoza took it over post-World War II).

TP—Proletarian Tendency of the FSLN.

UCA—Central American University, Managua.

UDEL—Democratic Union of Liberation (a liberal alternative political coalition which opposed Somoza; led by Pedro Joaquin Chamorro.

SPANISH WORDS

barrio—an urban neighborhood, usually poor but not necessarily a slum.

campesino(a)—"peasant," but with a broader meaning implying anyone from the countryside.

caudillo—a horse-back riding landlord or military leader; one who owns a ranch or rules a country or region.

companero(a)—close friend, intimate companion. May refer to either friendship, sexual liaison, or political comrade.

cordoba—Nicaraguan currency; one cordoba equals ten cents 1979 U.S. currency;

coup d'etat—overthrow of government or ruling body; in Spanish, "*golpe.*"

empresa—enterprise or industry.

foco—a small guerilla band, usually operating in the mountains.

hectare—metric unit of land, 1 hectare equals 2.3 acres.

junta—a board or governing body of either a national government or specific organization, as in "military *junta.*"

muchachos(as)—young boys and/or girls; those who fought in the streets against Somoza (from 7-15 years of age), especially during the September insurrection.

orejas—so-called "ears" or spies of Somoza.

¡presente!—an exclamation meaning "present," signifying that although someone has died in the struggle for justice and liberation, he or she is still alive in spirit.

somocismo—refers to a continuation of the structures and friends of Somoza in power even though Somoza himself might leave the country.

sandinismo—the spirit of Sandino in the Nicaraguan people; a political perspective that opposed the Somoza dynasty and U.S. imperialism; Nicarguan nationalism.

terceristas—see "Insurrectionalists."

TITLES OF ORGANIZATIONS OR PERSONS

Agro-Inra—Project of the Agrarian Reform Institute which manages state farms (post-victory).

Barricada—Official FSLN newspaper (post-victory).

Carlos Fonseca Amador—One of the three founders of the FSLN and the ideologue who insisted that the word "Sandinista" be included in the title of the Front.

Insurrection—Usually refers to the September Insurrection of 1978.

Insurrectionalists—a third FSLN tendency founded outside Nicaragua; sometimes referred to as the *terceristas*.

Internal Front—refers to the urban civilian forces during the final FSLN offensive in 1979.

Monimbo—an indigenous Indian neighborhood in the city of Masaya where the people first rose up in resistance to Somoza's National Guard and physically took control of their community.

National Guard—the U.S.-created and equipped armed forces of Somoza.

National Patriotic Front—Interim political organization created by the FSLN and the MPU in January 1979 as an alternative and a political challenge to the FAO.

Non-Aligned—those nations not aligned to the super powers (United States, Russia or China); usually Third World countries which are experimenting with different forms of mixed (i.e. capitalist and socialist) economies.

Novedades—Somoza's newspaper.

Obando y Bravo—(Mons. Miguel), Archbishop of Mangua.

Pro-Campo—service agency of INRA providing assistance and

advice to small peasant farmers.

La Prensa—opposition liberal newspaper; its founder and editor was Pedro Joaquin Chamorro.

Radio Sandino—clandestine FSLN radio station operating in Costa Rica during the struggle; official radio station of the Government of National Reconstruction and FSLN (post-victory).

Sandinista—a follower of Sandino; more specifically, a member or sympathizer of the FSLN.

Sandino—Augusto Cesar Sandino, "General of Free Men," led a peasant army and fought against the U.S. Marines, 1927-1933; assassinated by Somoza Garcia in 1934.

Trinational Commission—a commission created by the OAS at the urging of the United States in October 1978; made up of the United States, Guatemala and the Dominican Republic. Its task was to mediate between Somoza and the opposition after the Insurrection, seeking an alternative to Somoza.

The Twelve—twelve progressive liberal leaders who supported the FSLN and opposed the Somoza regime.

Unidades Estatales—State Entities; project of INRA which manages state-owned lands not involving industrial processing components (post-victory).